Man's Search for Ultimate Meaning

Viktor E. Frankl

**With a Foreword by Claudia Hammond
and
Afterword by Alexander Batthyány**

RIDER

LONDON · SYDNEY · AUCKLAND · JOHANNESBURG

9 10 8

This new edition with additional material first published in 2011 by Rider,
an imprint of Ebury Publishing
Ebury Publishing is a Random House Group company

Originally published in 2000 in the United States of America
by Perseus Publishing

The Random House Group Limited Reg. No. 954009

Addresses for companies within the Random House Group can be found at
www.randomhouse.co.uk

A CIP catalogue record for this book is available from the British Library

Penguin Random House is committed to a sustainable future for
our business, our readers and our planet. This book is made from
Forest Stewardship Council® certified paper.

MIX
Paper from
responsible sources
FSC® C018179

Printed and bound in Great Britain by Clays Ltd, St Ives plc

ISBN 9781846043062

Copies are available at special rates for bulk orders. Contact the sales
development team on 020 7840 8487 for more information

To buy books by your favourite authors and register for offers, visit
www.randomhouse.co.uk

VIKTOR E. FRANKL was Professor of Neurology and Psychiatry at the Uni. ... Medical School. For twenty-five years he was head of the Vienna Neurological Policlinic. His Logotherapy/Existential Analysis came to be known as the Third Viennese School of Psychotherapy. He held professorships at Harvard, Stanford, Dallas, and Pittsburgh, and was Distinguished Professor of Logotherapy at the US International University in San Diego, California. His writings have been called 'the most important contributions in the field of Psychotherapy since the days of Freud, Adler and Jung' by Sir Cyril Burt, ex-President of the British Psychological Society.

Born in 1905, Frankl received the degrees of Doctor of Medicine and Doctor of Philosophy from the University of Vienna. During World War II he spent three years at Auschwitz, Dachau and other concentration camps.

Through four decades Dr. Frankl made innumerable lecture tours throughout the world. He received honorary degrees from twenty-nine universities in Europe, the Americas, Africa and Asia. He held numerous awards, among them the Oskar Pfister Award of the American Psychiatric Association and an Honorary Membership of the Austrian Academy of Sciences.

Frankl's thirty-nine books appeared in thirty-eight languages. His book *Man's Search for Meaning* has sold millions of copies around the world. Viktor Frankl died in 1997 in Vienna.

"Viktor Frankl . . . is one of the moral heroes of the twentieth century. His insights into human freedom, dignity and the search for meaning are deeply humanising and have the power to transform lives" Chief Rabbi Dr Jonathan Sacks

"Viktor Frankl declares that evil and ennui cannot fully extinguish us" Brian Keenan, author of *An Evil Cradling*

ALSO BY VIKTOR E. FRANKL

Man's Search for Meaning
The Doctor and the Soul
Psychotherapy and Existentialism
The Will to Meaning
The Unconscious God
The Unheard Cry for Meaning

FOR MORE INFORMATION

Institutes of Logotherapy can now be found on all five
continents. For further information on Viktor Frankl and
Logotherapy, including an extensive bibliography, please
refer to the website of the Viktor Frankl Institute, Vienna
at www.viktorfrankl.org.

Contents

To my sister

Foreword by Claudia Hammond

As the title suggests, *Man's Search for Ultimate Meaning* is for anyone who is interested in the hunt for meaning in life. In it, Frankl explains how anyone can find meaning, whatever their circumstances, and why even a life of unbearable pain can still be meaningful. As people begin to wonder whether consumerism is really the way forward, at the start of the twenty-first century this book feels especially relevant.

I'm approaching writing this foreword in the way I imagine most people will approach reading the book—as an admirer of Victor Frankl's more famous work, *Man's Search for Meaning*. I still remember sitting in a café, making cups of tea last long enough for me to finish that book in the same afternoon. If you have not read the original no doubt you will want to by the time you have read this fascinating work.

Man's Search for Meaning, Frankl's meditation on suffering and survival, is a classic which has sold more than a million copies for each of the nine days he spent writing it (with sales now in excess of twelve million copies worldwide). We marvel at this concentrated genius, but those nine days only covered the act of writing his thoughts down; the thinking had taken place over many years. Like many great books, it left me wanting more. Some eminent writers leave us to gain all our understanding from the work alone, but with Frankl we are lucky enough to have the set of writings published here, in *Man's Search for Ultimate Meaning*, in which he explains his thinking in more depth. The following chapters undoubtedly have a unique value if read alone, but also provide a fresh perspective on and a new motivation for reading the first book again.

The second decade of the twenty-first century with its air of crisis and uncertainty is the perfect time to revisit Frankl's theories. Reading these writings by Frankl, I am struck many times by the way they anticipate modern research in the field of psychology. Here, he talks of tragic optimism, of how we know that life brings pain, guilt and death and yet, for the most part, we manage to carry on. Using his observations and experiences from the Holocaust, Frankl tells us how to deal with these three inevitable elements of life by making use of them: turn suffering into achievement, use guilt to improve yourself and use the knowledge that life is short as a spur to action. Half a century later optimism has become a key theme in the increasing influential field of positive psychology, the study of the strengths and virtues that allow both individuals and communities to thrive. Although I doubt Frankl would have described himself as associated with this field, there are some striking parallels.

Anyone with experience of cognitive behavioural therapy (CBT), either as a practitioner or a client, will see precursors of today's techniques in Frankl's work. In CBT, people learn how to reframe information, to find other ways of looking at their thoughts. In *Man's Search for Ultimate Meaning*, Frankl gives the example of an older man devastated by the loss of his wife. The man is questioning why she had to die first, leaving him alone and grief-stricken in old age. Frankl advises him to think of his staying behind as a sacrifice. He has saved his wife from experiencing this grief herself and should view it as a gift to the person he loved most in the world.

In psychological research today resilience is an important theme. Rather than teach children to have high self-esteem regardless of achievement, we should foster the strength of character to handle setbacks in the future as well as successes. Although resilience is not a word Frankl uses often, I would argue that again he was ahead of his time here. In a sense his observations in the concentration camps were studies of resilience—not just of other people's, but of his own. Part of the fascination in reading Frankl's work is watching how he employs coping mechanisms to manage his own mental survival. He found meaning in his experiences of the Holocaust by taking the opportunity not only to observe human behaviour in a situation far more desperate than any psychologist could create in a laboratory, but also to make use of those insights.

The most challenging element of *Man's Search for Ultimate Meaning* for me is the emphasis on religion. Frankl defines religion in its broadest sense, but coming to the material without faith myself and from a background in contemporary psychology, my initial reaction was to baulk at the prominence he gives it. However, Frankl anticipates late twentieth-century research on the potential of religion to aid recovery from mental health problems. While I would disagree with his view that only psychiatrists possessing religious feelings of their own can do this, there have been recent calls for mental health professionals to have more training in discussing spirituality with clients. It is true that sometimes such discussions make practitioners feel uncomfortable. Frankl could be talking today when he describes patients feeling ashamed to mention their religion to their psychiatrists.

If you come to this book as religious person the six and seventh chapters might be of particular interest to you, but if you are not religious there is still plenty here for you. For me, the most thought-provoking parts of the book are the final chapters, in which Frankl examines the problem of meaninglessness. He discusses the choice between taking a job that pays well or one that brings your life meaning. These are questions with particular pertinence during the economic downturn and this is where his theories can have lessons for us all today. Frankl is convinced that even when all control appears to have been taken away from us, such as when facing death in a concentration camp, it is still possible to find meaning. Although few of us will experience any such horror, the existential vacuum of modern life that he describes will resonate with many today. As we wonder if there is life beyond consumerism in a time where trust between individuals is decreasing, he talks about finding shared meaning and a new sense of community.

What I most admire about Frankl is his compassion and generosity. He had the opportunity to leave Vienna before the war, yet he stayed behind to care for his parents despite the risks. He is never prescriptive and admits that his form of existential analysis, logotherapy, is no panacea. The aim of this form of therapy is to help people find meaning in life and it rests on the premise that however wretched a person's circumstances, meaning still can be found. Frankl seems to want people to find their own way. His appalling experiences could have led him to dismiss as trivial everyday complaints about the meaninglessness of our safe, comfortable lives. Instead he seems to understand that *any* of us can feel lonely, in despair and in desperate need of meaning. In this way he turned his own battle to understand what he witnessed into a great contribution to twentieth-century thought. At the same time he put his theories into practice in his own life by making his work be devoted to helping others fulfil their own search for meaning.

CLAUDIA HAMMOND

Claudia Hammond is an award-winning broadcaster, writer and lecturer in psychology. Using her specialist knowledge she has originated and presented numerous radio series on psychology and science, including the critically acclaimed landmark series *State of Mind*. She has appeared often on TV, discussing psychological research, and is on the part-time faculty at Boston University's London base where she lectures in health and social psychology. Her first book, *Emotional Rollercoaster—a journey through the science of feelings*, has been translated into six languages.

Foreword (2000)

On January 1, 1994, I stood at the top of the stairs at the embassy residence, a bit confused. The diminutive, white-haired man walking spryly toward me wasn't at all what I had expected. I shook the hand of Viktor Frankl, my guest, and told him, "I read your book 25 years ago, and I still remember it."

"Do you remember in your mind, or in your heart?" he asked.

"In my heart."

"That's good," he answered, as if bestowing a blessing.

Throughout the coming months, I came to rely on Professor Frankl as a confidant and an advisor. Whether the subject was U.S. foreign policy in Bosnia, family health problems, or my own personal and professional priorities, Viktor and Elly were my anchor, a vital source of wisdom. And when wisdom failed us all, they were my wellspring of comfort.

Their clarity was imparted with kindness, under-standing, and love. I was close enough to know of some of their own travails. And I wondered about their own source of strength.

This book holds an answer to that question. For in it, we see Viktor Frankl dealing with the finitude of his place within infinite possibility. He does not confuse his own limitations with ultimate limitation, nor does he mistake his own being with ultimate being.

There is also an extraordinary sense of tolerance in his thinking—a graciousness in his concession that our symbols for ultimate meaning only point to a reality we cannot experience directly. The concentration camps in which he suffered and in which his loved ones died were, after all, created to annihilate those who were different. And so Frankl leaves room for the breadth of human experience of the metaphysical.

Let God take on an anthropomorphic form for some. For others, let God be confused with the self. After all, ultimate meaning is certainly able to absorb the finitude of our attempts to understand and describe infinity.

But for Frankl, such tolerance does not imply a lack of judgment. For there is evil in the world, and his life bears the scars. The unconscious search for ultimate meaning can lead to nefarious ends: flagrant nationalism, obsessive jealousies, ethnic hate, compulsive work. Half a century since this volume was conceived, I spent an afternoon with Elly and Viktor speaking not only of Auschwitz, but also of Srebrenica: a diabolic and perverted meaning found by some in sadistic debauchery.

So we are reminded once again that abstract theory is not an end in itself. It must shape concrete living. From this small volume, there is a great moral imperative to be pondered. As we reflect on Frankl's thought, we may take time to muse on what we personally hold most dear and, even in the moment of that intimate dialogue, contribute to the universal force for goodness.

Tolerance, jealousy, benevolence, hate, decency. What will be ultimate in our lives? As Viktor Frankl would remind us, the choice is ours.

Swanee Hunt
United States Ambassador
to Austria

Preface

The main title of this book is identical with the title of the Oskar Pfister Award Lecture that I gave at the annual meeting of the American Psychiatric Association in 1985. The text of this lecture is reprinted here as Chapter 9. As for the first part of this volume, it has already been published under the title "The Unconscious God" in 1975, the English translation of "Der unbewusste Gott," published in 1947. This book, in turn, had been based on the manuscript for a presentation I had been invited to give in Vienna, only a few months after the end of the war.

The "printing history" of the present volume thus goes back some 50 years. Perusing what I wrote in 1947, in 1975, and in 1985, I feel that it is, as a whole, a consistent sequence of presentations of some substantial thoughts regarding a quite important subject. Hopefully, then, some of what I have written throughout these decades may be of value to some readers.

However it may be—"See, I have not kept my lips closed."

V.F.

Preface to the First English Edition

The material in this book is drawn from a lecture I gave shortly after World War II, at the invitation of a small club of Viennese intellectuals. My audience was composed of no more than a dozen listeners. In 1947 the lecture was published as a book in German. It is only now, 28 years after its original publication, that the book appears in an English translation. (Spanish, Danish, Dutch, French, Greek, Hebrew, Italian, Japanese, Polish, Serbo-Croatian, and Swedish editions have already been published.)

Considering the time that has elapsed since the first edition—more than a quarter of a century—it might be understood that I no longer am in a position to subscribe fully to each and every word as it was printed in 1947. My thinking has developed considerably in the meantime—developed and, I hope, also matured.

To be sure, some of the changes have been implemented in the present edition by slightly altering certain passages. However, I have deliberately refrained from major alterations of the text because, of my 20 books, this is the most organized and systematized one, and it would have been a pity to destroy the cohesive structure of this piece of work by interspersing too much of the material that might have accrued in the meantime.

All the more, I welcomed the alternative that the publishers Simon and Schuster offered me, namely, to add, by way of a postscript, a supplementary chapter outlining some of the ideas that have evolved in my theory of conscience during the last two decades. As to the wider field that this book concerns, i.e., the interrelationship between psychotherapy and theology, the reader will find pertinent discussions in my two most recent books published in English (and in English only), *Psychotherapy and Existentialism*[*] and *The Will to Meaning.*[†] In each of these books one chapter explicitly deals with religious issues, and there are scattered references to this topic as well.

The updated bibliography at the end of this volume will enable the reader to locate further publications, not only those dealing with the relationship between religion and psychiatry but also those covering the whole area of logotherapeutic teachings and practices.

However, the main thesis propounded in the lecture entitled "The Unconscious God" remains still valid and tenable. There is, in fact, a religious sense deeply rooted in each and every man's unconscious depths. In two of my books, *Man's Search for Meaning*[‡] and the above-mentioned *The Will to Meaning*, evidence has been advanced to support my contention that this sense may

---

[*] Viktor E. Frankl, *Psychotherapy and Existentialism: Selected Papers on Logotherapy* (New York: Washington Square Press, 1967, and Touchstone Paperback, 1968).

[†] Viktor E. Frankl, *The Will to Meaning: Foundations and Applications of Logotherapy* (New York and Cleveland: The World Publishing Company, 1969; paperback edition, New York: New American Library, 1970).

[‡] Viktor E. Frankl, *Man's Search for Meaning: An Introduction to Logotherapy* (Boston: Beacon Press, 1959; New York: Touchstone, Simon and Schuster, 1973).

break through unexpectedly, even in cases of severe mental illness such as psychoses. For example, a student of mine at the United States International University, San Diego, California, wrote:

> In the mental hospital, I was locked like an animal in a cage, no one came when I called begging to be taken to the bathroom, and I finally had to succumb to the inevitable. Blessedly, I was given daily shock treatment, insulin shock, and sufficient drugs so that I lost most of the next several weeks. . . .

> But in the darkness I had acquired a sense of my own unique mission in the world. I knew then, as I know now, that I must have been preserved for some reason—however small, it is something that only I can do, and it is vitally important that I do it. And because in the darkest moment of my life, when I lay abandoned as an animal in a cage, when because of the forgetfulness induced by ECT I *could not call* out to Him, He was there. In the solitary darkness of the "pit" where men had abandoned me, *He was there.* When I did not know His Name, He was there; God was there.

Likewise, such unexpected religious feelings may break through under other circumstances, as was the case with a man who wrote from prison:

> I am at the age of 54 financially ruined, in jail. At the beginning of this incarceration (8 months ago) everything looked hopeless and irrevocably lost in chaos that I could never hope to understand, much less to solve.

> Endless months passed. Then, one day I had a visit by a court psychiatrist to whom I took an immense liking, right from the start, as he introduced himself with a very pleasant smile and a handshake, like I would be still "somebody," or at least a human being. Something deep and unexplainable happened to me from there on. I found myself reliving my life. That night, in the stillness of my small cell, I experienced a most unusual religious feeling which I never had before; I was able

to pray, and with utmost sincerity, I accepted a Higher Will to which I have surrendered the pain and sorrow as meaningful and ultimate, not needing explanation. From here on I have undergone a tremendous recovery.

This happened in Baltimore County Prison in April of this year. Today, I am at complete peace with myself and the world. I have found the true meaning of my life, and time can only delay its fulfillment but not deter it. At fifty-four, I have decided to reconstruct my life and to finish my schooling. I am sure I can accomplish my goal. I have also found a new great source of unexpected vitality—I am able now to laugh over my own miseries, instead of wallowing in the pain of irrevocable failure, and somehow there are hardly any great tragedies left. . . .

But one may discuss religion irrespective of whether it is unconscious or conscious, for the question confronting us is more basic and radical. First, we must ask ourselves whether this is a legitimate area for psychiatric exploration. Lately, I have come to draw the line of demarcation between religion and psychiatry ever more sharply.* I have learned, and taught, that the difference between them is no more nor less than a difference between various dimensions. From the very analogy with dimensions, however, it should become clear that these realms are by no means mutually exclusive. A higher dimension, by definition, is a more *inclusive one.* The lower dimension is included in the higher one; it is subsumed in it and encompassed by it. Thus biology is overarched by psychology, psychology by noölogy, and noölogy by theology.

The noölogical dimension may rightly be defined as the dimension of uniquely human phenomena. Among them, there is one that I regard as the most representative

* Viktor E. Frankl, *The Doctor and the Soul: From Psychotherapy to Logotherapy.* (New York: Alfred A. Knopf, Inc.; second, expanded edition, 1965; paperback edition, New York: Vintage Books, 1973).

of the human reality. I have circumscribed this phenomenon in terms of "man's search for meaning." Now, if this is correct, one may also be justified in defining religion as man's search for *ultimate* meaning. It was Albert Einstein who once contended that to be religious is to have found an answer to the question, What is the meaning of life? If we subscribe to this statement we may then define belief and faith as *trust* in ultimate meaning. Once we have conceived of religion in this way—that is, in the widest possible sense—there is no doubt that psychiatrists are entitled also to investigate this phenomenon, although only its human aspect is accessible to a psychological exploration.

The concept of religion in its widest possible sense, as it is here espoused, certainly goes far beyond the narrow concepts of God promulgated by many representatives of denominational and institutional religion. They often depict, not to say denigrate, God as a being who is primarily concerned with being believed in by the greatest possible number of believers, and along the lines of a specific creed, at that. "Just believe," we are told, "and everything will be okay." But alas, not only is this order based on a distortion of any sound concept of deity, but even more importantly it is doomed to failure: Obviously, there are certain activities that simply cannot be commanded, demanded, or ordered, and as it happens, the triad "faith, hope, and love" belongs to this class of activities that elude an approach with, so to speak, "command characteristics." Faith, hope, and love cannot be established by command simply because they cannot be established at will. I cannot "will" to believe, I cannot "will" to hope, I cannot "will" to love—and least of all can I "will" to will.

Upon closer investigation it turns out that what underlies the attempt to establish faith, hope, love, and will by command is the manipulative approach. The attempt to bring these states about at will, however, is ultimately based on an inappropriate objectification and reification of these human phenomena: They are turned into mere things, into mere objects. However, since faith, hope, love, and will are so-called "intentional" acts or activities, along the lines of the terminology coined by Edmund Husserl and Max Scheler, the founders of the school of "phenomenology," these activities are directed to "intentional" referents—in other words, to objects of their own. To the extent that one makes intentional acts into objects, he loses sight of *their* objects. Nowhere, to my knowledge, is this brought home to us more strikingly than with the uniquely human phenomenon of laughter: You cannot order anyone to laugh—if you want him to laugh, you must tell him a joke.

But isn't it, in a way, the same with religion? If you want people to have faith and belief in God, you cannot rely on preaching along the lines of a particular church but must, in the first place, portray your God believably—and you must act credibly yourself. In other words, you have to do the very opposite of what so often is done by the representatives of organized religion when they build up an image of God as someone who is primarily interested in being believed in and who rigorously insists that those who believe in him be affiliated with a particular church. Small wonder that such representatives of religion behave as though they saw the main task of their own denomination as that of overriding other denominations.

Certainly the trend is away from religion conceived in such a strictly denominational sense. Yet this is not to imply that, eventually, there will be a universal religion. On the contrary, if religion is to survive, it will have to be profoundly personalized.

This does not mean that there is no need for symbols and rituals. Even the die-hard agnostic and atheist cannot completely dismiss symbols. Consider the Russians, who once constructed a monument to express symbolically their indebtedness and gratitude to the thousands of dogs that had been sacrificed by Pavlov in the course of his famous conditioned-reflex experiments—what a purely symbolic gesture, pointless by the utilitarian yardstick adopted by dialectical materialism, and yet extremely meaningful to the heart of the Russian nation. A heart like that, as Blaise Pascal once observed, has reasons that are unknown to reason (*le coeur a ses raisons que la raison ne connaît point*). The heart of man defies even Marxist indoctrination.

To all appearances, religion is not dying, and insofar as this is true, God is not dead either, not even "after Auschwitz," to quote the title of a book. For either belief in God is unconditional or it is not belief at all. If it is unconditional it will stand and face the fact that six million died in the Nazi holocaust; if it is not unconditional it will fall away if only a single innocent child has to die—to resort to an argument once advanced by Dostoevski. There is no point in bargaining with God, say, by arguing: "Up to six thousand or even one million victims of the holocaust I maintain my belief in Thee; but from one million upward nothing can be done any longer, and I am sorry but I must renounce my belief in Thee."

The truth is that among those who actually went through the experience of Auschwitz, the number of those whose religious life was deepened—in spite of, not because of, this experience—by far exceeds the number of those who gave up their belief. To paraphrase what La Rochefoucauld once remarked with regard to love, one might say that just as the small fire is extinguished by the storm while a large fire is enhanced by it—likewise a weak faith is weakened by predicaments and catastrophes, whereas a strong faith is strengthened by them.

Viktor E. Frankl

Acknowledgments

When I first conceived the idea to expand one of my personally favorite works, *The Unconscious God*, into *Man's Search for Ultimate Meaning*, I thought it to be a rather uncomplicated task. As in all things, experience turned out to be the best teacher. Bringing this book to fruition has been truly a team effort, and for that I am indebted to many.

I am indebted to Joanna Lawrence of Plenum Publishing Company for making *Man's Search for Ultimate Meaning* a reality. I am also most grateful to the Honorable Swanee Hunt, the U.S. Ambassador to Austria, for honoring me by writing the Foreword to this book. She has captured the true spirit of my work. I am also indebted to Dr. Jay Levinson, my assistant and friend, for his help in coordinating the many logistical details of this project. I am deeply grateful to my son-in-law, Dr. Franz Vesely, who served as my personal "editor-in-chief" in Vienna, providing advice and help whenever it was needed. Without the diligent and gracious service of Franz and Jay this book would never have become a reality. Last, but certainly not least, I wish to express my love and appreciation to my wife, Elly. She is my light, my inspiration, my support.

To them and to all the other unnamed contributors I express my deepest appreciation.

Man's Search for Ultimate Meaning

ECCE LABIA MEA NON COHIBUI

CHAPTER 1

The Essence of Existential Analysis

Arthur Schnitzler, Vienna's famous poet and a contemporary of Sigmund Freud, has been quoted as saying that there are really only three virtues: objectivity, courage, and sense of responsibility. It would be tempting to allot to each of these virtues one of the schools of psychotherapy that have emerged from Viennese soil.

It is obvious that the virtue of courage fits Adlerian psychology. The Adlerian, after all, regards his entire therapeutic procedure, in the final analysis, as nothing but an attempt at encouraging the patient. The purpose of this encouragement is to help the patient overcome his inferiority feelings, which Adlerian psychology considers to be a decisive pathogenic factor.

In the same way, another of the virtues mentioned fits Freudian psychoanalysis—that of objectivity. What else could it have been that enabled Sigmund Freud, like Oedipus, to look into the eyes of the Sphinx-—the human *psyche*—and draw out its riddle at the risk of a most dreadful discovery? In his time such an undertaking was colossal, and so was his accomplishment. Up to then psychology, particularly so-called academic psychology, had shunned everything that Freud then made the focus of his teaching. As the anatomist Julius Tandler jokingly called the "somatology" that was taught in Vienna's junior high schools "anatomy with the exclusion of the genital," so Freud could have said that academic psychology was psychology with the exclusion of the libidinal.

However, psychoanalysis not only adopted objectivity—it succumbed to it. Objectivity eventually led to objectification, or reification. That is, psychoanalysis made the human person into an object, the human being into a thing. Psychoanalysis regards the patient as ruled by "mechanisms," and it conceives of the therapist as the one who knows the technique by which disturbed mechanisms may be repaired.

But cynicism lurks behind an interpretation of psychotherapy in terms of mere technique. It is true that we can see the therapist as a technician only if we have first viewed the patient as some sort of machine. Only an *homme machine*, I would say, is in need of a *médecin technicien*.

How is it that psychoanalysis arrived at this technically minded, mechanistic view? It is understandable considering the intellectual climate in which psychoanalysis emerged, but it must also be understood in the context of the social milieu of the time—a milieu full of prudery. The mechanistic view was a reactionary response to that prudery, and today it is out of date in many respects. But Freud not only reacted to his time, he also acted out of his time. When he formed his teaching he did so completely under the influence of associationism, which was then beginning to dominate the field of psychology. Associationism, however, was the product of naturalism, an ideology typical of the late nineteenth century. Within Freud's teaching naturalism makes itself most conspicuous in two basic characteristics of psychoanalysis: its psychological atomism and its theory of psychic energy.

Psychoanalysis views the whole of the human psyche atomistically as pieced together out of separate parts, i.e., out of various drives, which in turn are composed of so-called drive components. Thus the psyche is not only atomized but an-atomized, i.e., the analysis of the psyche becomes its anatomy. In this way, the wholeness of the human person is destroyed. One could say, on the one hand, that psychoanalysis depersonalizes man. On the other hand, it personifies the individual aspects within the totality of the psyche, aspects that are often in conflict with one another. Sometimes they are not only personified but even demonized, e.g., when the id or the superego is dealt with as if it were a relatively independent, pseudo-personal power in itself.

Psychoanalysis destroys the unified whole of the human person, and then has the task of reconstructing the whole person out of the pieces. This atomistic view is most evident in Freud's hypothesis that the ego is made up out of "ego drives." According to this hypothesis the censor, which represses the drives, is itself a drive. Just consider the following statement from Freud's *Three Essays on the Theory of Sexuality:*" . . . the production of sexual excitation . . . produces a store of energy which is employed to a great extent for purposes other than sexual—namely . . . (through repression . . .) in building up the subsequently developed barriers against sexuality."[1] To me this is comparable to claiming that a builder who has constructed a building out of bricks is himself built of bricks, for that which builds a barrier against sexuality cannot itself be made up of sexuality. What is obvious here is the materialism that permeates the psychoanalytic way of thinking and also ultimately accounts for its atomism.

In addition to atomism, psychoanalysis is characterized by energism. Psychoanalysis, in fact, operates constantly with the concepts of instinctual energism and emotional dynamism. Drives as well as drive components work the same way as what physics call a "parallelogram of forces." But on what are these forces working? The answer is the ego. The ego in the psychoanalytic view is ultimately a plaything of the drives. Or as Freud himself once said, the ego is not the master in its own house.

Psychological phenomena are therefore reduced to drives and instincts and thus seem to be totally determined, i.e., caused, by them. Being human is a priori interpreted by psychoanalysis in terms of being driven. That is also the ultimate reason why the ego, once it has been dismembered, has to be reconstructed out of the drives.

Possessed of such an atomistic, energistic, and mechanistic concept of man, psychoanalysis sees him in the final analysis as the automaton of a psychic apparatus. And that is precisely the point where existential analysis comes in. It pits a different concept of man against the psychoanalytic one. It is not focused on the automaton of a psychic apparatus but rather on the autonomy of spiritual existence. ("Spiritual" is used here without any religious connotation, of course, but rather just to indicate that we are dealing with a specifically human phenomenon, in contrast to the phenomena that we share with other animals. In other words, the "spiritual" is what is human in man.)

And thus we come back to Schnitzler's list of virtues. Just as we could apply the virtue of objectivity to psychoanalysis and that of courage to Adlerian psychology, so it is apt to apply to existential analysis the virtue of responsibility. In fact, existential analysis interprets human existence, and indeed being human, ultimately in terms of being responsible. At the time we introduced the term "existential analysis"[2] in 1938, contemporary philosophy offered the word "existence" to denote that specific mode of being that is basically characterized by being responsible.

If we were to give a quick account of what led existential analysis to recognize responsibleness as the essence of existence, then we would have to begin with an inversion of the question, What is the meaning of life? I made this inversion in my first book, *Ärztliche Seelsorge*,[3] when I contended that man is not he who poses the question, What is the meaning of life? but he who is asked this question, for it is life itself that poses it to him. And man has to answer to life by answering for life; he has to respond by being responsible; in other words, the response is necessarily a response-in-action.

While we respond to life "in action" we are also responding in the "here and now." What is always involved in our response is the concreteness of a person and the concreteness of the situation in which he is involved. Thus our responsibility is always responsibility *ad personam* plus *ad situationem*.

Existential analysis, in the form of logotherapy, is a psychotherapeutic method because it is concerned, in particular, with the neurotic mode of being and is intended to bring man—the neurotic, in particular—to an awareness of his responsibleness. As in psychoanalysis, so in existential analysis man becomes conscious of something. But whereas in psychoanalysis it is the instinctual of which he becomes conscious, in existential analysis, or logotherapy, he becomes conscious of the spiritual, or existential. For it is only from the viewpoint of man's spirituality, or existentiality, that being human can be described in terms of being responsible. What comes to consciousness in existential analysis, then, is not drive or instinct, neither id drives nor ego drives, but self. Here it is not the ego that becomes conscious of the id but rather the self that becomes conscious of itself.

CHAPTER 2

The Spiritual Unconscious

We now arrive at an essential revision of the prevalent concept of the unconscious, or more specifically, of its extent. We have to expand its limits because it turns out that there is not only an instinctual unconscious but a spiritual unconscious as well. Thus the content of the unconscious has been differentiated into unconscious instinctuality and unconscious spirituality.

Previously we have tried to supplement psychotherapy in the strict sense of the word by introducing logotherapy as a psychotherapy centered and focusing on the spiritual—which constitutes the noölogical dimension as distinct from the psychological dimension. Having thus included the spiritual into psychology in general, we now include it in particular into depth psychology—that is, into the psychology of the unconscious.

Freud saw only unconscious instinctuality, as represented in what he called the id; to him the unconscious was first and foremost a reservoir of repressed instinctuality. However, the spiritual may also be unconscious; moreover, existence is *essentially* unconscious, because the foundation of existence cannot be fully reflected upon and thus cannot be fully aware of itself.

Since the instinctual and the spiritual are both unconscious, and the spiritual may be conscious as well as unconscious, we now have to ask ourselves how sharp these two distinctions are. The border between the conscious and the unconscious is a very fluid one—it is permeable—for there is a constant transition from one to the other. We need only consider what psychoanalysis has termed repression: In the act of repression something conscious becomes unconscious; vice versa, in the removal of repression something unconscious is made conscious again.

In contrast to the "fluid" border between the conscious and the unconscious, the line between the spiritual and the instinctual cannot be drawn sharply enough. This fact has been expressed most concisely by Ludwig Binswanger when he spoke of "instincts and spirit" as "incommensurable concepts." Since human existence is spiritual existence, we now see that the distinction between conscious and unconscious becomes unimportant compared with another distinction: The real criterion of authentically human existence derives from discerning whether a given phenomenon is spiritual or instinctual, whereas it is relatively irrelevant whether it is conscious or unconscious. This is due to the fact that—in contrast to the psychoanalytic concept—being human is not being driven but "deciding what one is going to be," to quote Jaspers *(entscheidendes Sein)*, or to quote Heidegger: *Dasein*. I would say that being human is being responsible—existentially responsible, responsible for one's own existence.

Existence thus may well be authentic even when it is unconscious, but man exists authentically only when he is not driven but, rather, responsible. Authentic existence is present where a self is deciding for itself, but not where an id is driving it.

It might be said that psychoanalysis has "id-ified," and "de-self-ified," human existence. Insofar as Freud degraded the self to a mere epiphenomenon, he betrayed the self and delivered it to the id; at the same time, he denigrated the unconscious, in that he saw in it only the instinctual and overlooked the spiritual.

Before, we stated that the line between the spiritual—as the human in man—and the instinctual cannot be drawn sharply enough. In fact we may conceive of it as an ontological hiatus that separates the two fundamentally distinct regions within the total structure of the human being. On one side is existence, and on the other side is whatever belongs to facticity: Whereas existence, according to our definition, is in essence spiritual, facticity contains somatic and psychic "facts," the physiological as well as the psychological. And whereas the line between existence and facticity, that ontological hiatus, must be drawn as sharply as possible, within the realm of facticity the line between the somatic and the psychic cannot be drawn clearly. Any physician who has ever tried to elucidate the multidimensional etiology of a psycho-somatic condition knows very well how difficult it is to differentiate between psychogenic and somatogenic components.

As the dichotomy "conscious-unconscious" has become only a secondary issue, so the age-old psycho-physical problem now proves to have lost its primary significance. It has to recede behind the much more essential problem of spiritual existence versus psycho-physical facticity. This issue is not only a problem of greater ontological import, but also one of greater psycho-therapeutic relevancy. After all, a psychotherapist is continually concerned with spiritual existence in terms of freedom and responsibility, and with marshaling it against the psychophysical facticity that the patient is prone to accept as his fate. The awareness of freedom and respon-sibleness that constitutes authentic humanness must be set against this neurotic fatalism.

But we must not neglect the fact that being human is always individualized being. As such, it is always centered around a core, and this core is the person, who, in the words of Max Scheler, is not only the agent but also the "center" of spiritual activity. I would say that this spiritual personal center is encompassed by the peripheral psychophysical layers. Now instead of talking of spiritual existence and psychophysical facticity, we may speak of the spiritual person and "its" psychophysical overlay. By "its" we mean to emphasize that the person "has" a psychophysical overlay, whereas the person "is" spiritual. After all, I am not really justified in saying "my self," not even "myself," since I do not "have" a self, but I "am" a self. If anything, I can "have" an id, but precisely in the sense of psychophysical facticity.

By being centered around the existential, personal, spiritual core, being human is not only individualized but also integrated. Thus the spiritual core, and only the spiritual core, warrants and constitutes oneness and wholeness in man. Wholeness in this context means the integration of somatic, psychic, and spiritual aspects. It is not possible to overstate that it is this threefold wholeness that makes man complete. In no way are we justified in speaking of man as only a "somatic-psychic whole." Body and psyche may form a unity—a psychophysical unity—but this unity does not yet represent the wholeness of man. Without the spiritual as its essential ground, this wholeness cannot exist. As long as we speak only of body and psyche, wholeness has eluded us.

As far as the structure of the human being is concerned, we have so far given preference to the model of layers versus the model of strata. In fact, we have replaced the vertical hierarchy of unconscious, preconscious, and conscious strata with the model of concentric layers, a model propounded by Max Scheler.

But why not go one step further by combining the strata model with the layers model? Why not conceive of the concentric layers as the ground plan of a three-dimensional structure? We would only have to imagine

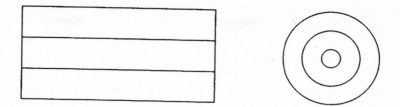

that the personal core—the spiritual center that is encompassed by the peripheral somatic and psychic layers—is prolonged so that we would have to conceive of it as an axis. This axis then would extend, together with the peripheral layers encompassing it, throughout the unconscious, preconscious, and conscious strata.

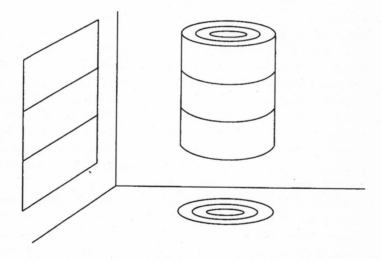

In other words, we have put together two two-dimensional models and made them into a three-dimensional one. Now the two former models have been reconciled, as it were, having become the two-dimensional projections of a three-dimensional model that more accurately depicts the human reality we are describing.

Any human phenomenon, whether belonging to the personal axis or to the somatic-psychic layers, may occur on any level: the unconscious, preconscious, or conscious.

To take up once more the issue of "depth psychology" we have to extend the meaning of this concept, because up to now depth psychology has followed man into the depth of his instincts, but too little into the depth of his spirit. Since "depth" refers to the unconscious, it necessarily follows that the person in his depth, the spirit in its depth, or, for that matter, human existence in its depth is essentially unconscious. This is due to the fact that spiritual activity so absorbs the person as the executor of spiritual acts that he is not even capable of reflecting on what he basically is. The self does not yield to total self-reflection.[1] In this sense, human existence is basically unreflectable, and so is the self in itself. Human existence exists in action rather than reflection.

Insofar as human existence cannot fully be reflected upon by itself, it cannot be fully analyzed either. That is why existential analysis can never be an analysis of existence but only an analysis toward existence. Human existence remains an *Urphänomen*, i.e., an unanalyzable, irreducible phenomenon. And this holds for each of its basic aspects, e.g., such human phenomena as consciousness and responsibleness. If these are to be illuminated, we have to transcend the ontic plane toward the ontological dimension. Within the plane of psychological immanence, both consciousness and responsibleness are and remain unsolvable problems. However, as soon as we transpose them into the ontological dimension they cease to be problems. For then they are taken as *Urphänomene*, constitutive of human existence, or in Heideggerian terms, they are "existentials," attributes that belong to the very foundations of human existence.

To sum up, spiritual phenomena may be unconscious or conscious; the spiritual basis of human existence, however, is ultimately unconscious. Thus the center of the human person in his very depth is unconscious. In its origin, the human spirit is unconscious spirit.

Precisely at the place of its origin, the retina of the eye has a "blind spot," where the optic nerve enters the eyeball. Likewise, the spirit is "blind" precisely at its origin—precisely there, no self-observation, no mirroring of itself is possible; where the spirit is "original" spirit, where it is fully itself, precisely there it is also unconscious of itself. We may therefore fully subscribe to what has been said in the Indian Vedas: "That which does the seeing, cannot be seen; that which does the hearing, cannot be heard; and that which does the thinking, cannot be thought."

However, the spirit is unconscious not only where it originates, that is, in its depth, but also in its height. In fact, that which has to decide whether something is to be conscious or unconscious is itself unconscious. Just consider the fact that there is something in the sleeping man that decides whether or not he should continue sleeping. This guard, for example, has the sleeping mother awake as soon as the breathing of her child becomes irregular, whereas she sleeps through loud noises from the street. Even in states of hypnosis this guard does not fail— the subject wakes up as soon as he becomes uncomfortable with the hypnotic suggestion. Only in deeper states of narcosis is this guard put to silence—put to sleep itself. Otherwise it keeps watch over man as if it were conscious, and yet it is at best quasiconscious. True, it somehow must know what happens around the sleeper, but this has nothing to do with actual consciousness. That which decides whether an experience will become conscious or will remain unconscious is itself unconscious. In order to make such a decision, however, it must somehow be able to discern. Since both deciding and discerning are spiritual acts, again it follows that these spiritual acts not only can be, but must be, unconscious—unconscious and unreflectable.

CHAPTER 3

Existential Analysis of Conscience

The phenomenon of conscience serves well as a model to further illuminate our concept of the spiritual unconscious. As we said in the preceding chapter, conscience, along with responsibleness, is a true *Urphänomen,* an irreducible phenomenon that is inherent in the human being as a deciding being, as *entscheidendes Sein.* Now whatever we have previously attempted to derive theoretically must let itself be shown phenomenologically through the medium of the phenomenon of conscience. In fact, conscience reaches down into unconscious depths and stems from an unconscious ground; it is precisely those momentous, authentic—existentially authentic—decisions that take place completely without reflection and thus unconsciously. Precisely where it originates, conscience delves down into the unconscious.

In this sense conscience is irrational; it is alogical or, better put, prelogical. Just as there is a prescientific understanding and, ontologically even prior to it, a prelogical understanding of being, so there is a premoral understanding of meaning, and this is conscience. The premoral understanding of meaning precedes any understanding of values, and therefore is not contingent upon morals.

In which sense may we regard conscience as being irrational? At least while in action it can never be explained in rational terms; such explanation is possible only "after the fact." Moral self-scrutiny also is possible only afterward. The judgments of conscience, in the final analysis, are inscrutable.

If we ask ourselves why conscience necessarily operates in an irrational way, then we have to consider the following. What is disclosed to consciousness is something that *is*; however, what is revealed to conscience is not anything that is but, rather, something that *ought to be*. What merely ought to be is not real, but is something to make real; it is no actuality but mere possibility (although in a higher, ethical sense, such a possibility again represents a necessity). Insofar as that which has been disclosed to conscience is still to be actualized, the question emerges how it could be realized unless it were somehow anticipated in the first place. Such anticipation, however, can only be enacted through intuition.

So conscience is essentially intuitive. To anticipate what is not yet, but is to be made real, conscience must be based on intuition. And it is in this sense that conscience may be called irrational. But is not conscience in this respect analogous to love? Is not love just as irrational, just as intuitive? In fact, love does intuit, for it also envisions something that is not yet real. What love anticipates, however, is not an ethical necessity but, rather, a personal possibility. Love reveals potentialities dormant in the loved person that he still has to make real.

However, concern with mere possibilities rather than actualities is not the only common denominator of love and conscience. It is one reason why both must operate on an intuitive level; a second reason is to be seen in the fact that both love and conscience have to do with something, or someone, absolutely unique.

It is the task of conscience to disclose to man the *unum necesse,* the one thing that is required. This one thing, however, is absolutely unique inasmuch as it is the unique possibility a concrete person has to actualize in a specific situation. What matters is the *unique* "ought to be" that cannot be comprehended by any universal law. No generally valid law in the sense of Immanuel Kant's "categorical imperative" can get hold of it, but only an "individual law" in the sense of Georg Simmel. And above all, it can never be comprehended in rational terms, but only intuitively.

Insofar as conscience intuitively discloses such concrete, individual possibilities of meaning, one might be tempted to think of the way conscience operates as instinctive, and thus to speak of conscience itself as an ethical instinct. But once we take a closer look we see that this ethical instinct markedly deviates from what generally is called instinct, i.e., the biological instinct, which operates through "innate releasing schemes," or "mechanisms," according to Konrad Lorenz. The instinctive reactions of animals to certain environmental signs and signals (*Merkmale* and *Wirkmale* according to von Uexküll) are strictly schematic and rigid for each species. The effectiveness of such schemes thus depends on the fact that they only work for the species in general, for the benefit of the greatest number, whereas in individual cases they not only fail but sometimes even mislead the animal to act "unwisely." The same instinctive pattern of reaction that preserves and saves, for example, the majority of ants may in a given case mean the destruction of a particular ant: The "wisdom" of the instincts requires that such a "sacrifice" be made for the sake of the whole ant colony. The vital instincts in principle neglect the individual.

The "ethical instinct" is entirely different. In contrast to vital instincts, the effectiveness of the ethical instinct depends on the fact that its target is not anything general but something individual, something concrete. And just as the animal is at times misled by the vital instincts, so may man go astray, ironically, by obeying the precepts of moral reason that, as such, deal only with generalities, whereas the ethical instinct alone enables him to discover the unique requirement of a unique situation, the *unum necesse*. Only conscience is capable of adjusting the "eternal," generally agreed-upon moral law to the specific situation in which a concrete person is engaged. Living one's conscience always means living on a highly personalized level, aware of the full concreteness of each situation. Indeed, conscience has comprehended the concrete "whereness" *(Da)* of my personal being *(Sein)* all along.

Love also parallels conscience with respect to the uniqueness of its target. Just as conscience aims at the uniqueness of possibilities dormant in each life situation, so love aims at the equally unique potentialities dormant in a loved person. Even more, love alone enables the loving person to grasp the uniqueness of the loved person. In this sense love has a significant cognitive function, and certainly this was appreciated by the ancient Hebrews when they used the same word for the act of love and the act of knowledge.

Are we also justified to compare the quality of deciding and choosing in love and in conscience? Does love even have to do with decision and choice? Certainly it does. To be sure, the choice of a partner is only a true choice when it is not dictated by drives. As long as, for example, an unconscious image, an "imago," determines my "choice," it cannot be a matter of love. And as long as a self is driven by an id to a Thou, it is not a matter of love, either. In love the self is not driven by the id, but rather the self chooses the Thou.

However, not only love and moral conscience are rooted in the emotional and intuitive, nonrational depths of the spiritual unconscious, but also what I would call the artistic conscience. Thus, ethics and aesthetics as well have their foundation and basis within the spiritual unconscious. In fact, in his creative work the artist is dependent on sources and resources deriving from the spiritual unconscious.[1] The nonrational intuition of conscience is paralleled by the inspiration of the artist. Artistic creation emerges out of recesses in a realm that can never be fully illuminated. We clinicians observe time and again that excessive reflection on the creative process proves to be harmful. Forced self-observation may become a severe handicap to the creativity of the artist. An attempt to produce on a conscious level what must grow in unconscious depths, the attempt to manipulate the primal creative process by reflecting on it, is doomed to failure. Reflection comes only later.

We know a case in which a violinist always tried to play as consciously as possible. From putting his violin in place on his shoulder to the most trifling technical detail, he wanted to do everything consciously, to perform in full self-reflection. This led to a complete artistic breakdown. Therapy had to start with eliminating this tendency to overbearing self-reflection and self-observation, or, in the terminology of logotherapy, "hyperreflection." Therapy had to be aimed at what we call in logotherapy "dereflection." Treatment had to give back to the patient his trust in the unconscious, by having him realize how much more musical his unconscious was than his conscious. As a matter of fact, this treatment oriented toward the patient's reliance on his unconscious brought about the release of the artistic "creative powers" of his unconscious. Dereflection liberated the creative process from the inhibiting effects of any unnecessary reflection.

This brings to the fore the question, What should be the goal of psychotherapy? No longer is one allowed to believe that the goal of psychotherapy consists in making something conscious at any price. Becoming conscious is no more than a transitory stage in the psychotherapeutic process. It has to make conscious the unconscious—including the spiritual unconsciouness—only in order to allow it finally to recede back to unconsciousness. To put it in the terms of the Scholastics, what therapy has to achieve is to convert an unconscious *potentia* into a conscious *actus*, but to do so for no other reason than to restore it eventually as an unconscious *habitus*. It is the task of the therapist, in the final analysis, to reinstate the spontaneity and naïveté of an unreflected existential act.

This might seem to imply that artistic creativity, or any spiritual activity, is just a matter of emotions and feelings. But the concept of emotion and feeling has today become too vague, and it is important to bear in mind Scheler's distinction between feeling as a mere "emotional state" *(Gefühlszustand)* and feeling as an "intentional feeling" *(intentionales Gefühl)*, i.e., a feeling directed to an intentional referent. As a matter of fact, such intentional feelings may well have their roots in the spiritual unconscious, but the mere emotional states have as little to do with spiritual existence as do any states caused by instinctual drives.

To say that the concept of feeling is vague in no way implies that feeling itself is vague. At least as far as "intentional feeling" is concerned, it is rather the contrary: Feeling can be much more sensitive than reason can ever be sensible.

The difficulties we run into when we try to explore the necessarily unconscious sources of spiritual activity are demonstrated by the fact, trivial as it might seem, that people have always made jokes and have laughed but there is still no full scientific explication of phenomena such as joking and laughing. This shows just how independent an act can be from any reflective understanding of it.

In conclusion, where the spiritual self steeps itself in its unconscious depths, there occur the phenomena of conscience, love, and art. Where it happens the other way around, however—that is to say, where the somatopsychic id intrudes into consciousness—there we have to deal with a neurosis or a psychosis, depending on whether the case is psychogenic or somatogenic.

CHAPTER 4

Existential Analysis of Dreams

From what has been discussed it seems to follow that the spiritual unconscious would be extremely difficult to illuminate. And yet there is a way by which the unconscious—including its spiritual aspect—yields itself to exploration, namely, by way of dreams. Since Freud introduced the classical method of dream interpretation, based on free associations, we have learned to avail ourselves of this technique. This is also done in existential analysis, although our goal is to lift not only instinctual but also spiritual phenomena into consciousness—and into responsibleness. After all, dreams, are the true creations of the unconscious, and therefore we may expect that not only elements of the instinctual unconscious will come to the fore, but elements of the spiritual unconscious as well. Thus we use the same method Freud did when he tracked down the instinctual unconscious, but we may use the method to a different end, the disclosure of the spiritual unconscious.

Conscience has proved to be an apt model to demonstrate how the spiritual unconscious operates. The same model now may well serve us in the context of dream analysis. To take an example:

A woman dreamed that, along with her dirty wash, she took a dirty cat to the laundry. When she came to pick up the laundry she found the cat dead. She came up with the following free associations: As to "cat," she said that she loved cats above all; but equally she loved her daughter— her only child—"above all." From this we may infer that "cat" stands for "child." But why is the cat "dirty"? That became clear as soon as we learned from the patient that recently she had been worrying about the gossip surrounding her daughter's love life—her "dirty linen," too, was being washed in public. That was the reason why the patient, as she admitted, was constantly watching and hounding her daughter. The dream therefore expressed a warning to the patient not to torment her daughter with exaggerated demands of moral "cleanliness" or she might lose her child.

We cannot see any reason why we should give up such a straightforward interpretation, open to whatever presents itself in the dream, in deference to the preconceived idea that behind it infantile sexual content *must* be hidden. The phenomena of the spiritual unconscious are empirical facts, and confronted with them, we wish to embrace the great virtue of psychoanalysis: objectivity. Such objectivity, however, should be demanded not only of the analysand but of the analyst as well. Just as unconditional honesty is required of the analysand, so the analyst should be equally honest and not close his eyes to the facts of the spiritual unconscious.

Consider the dream of another patient:

The patient reports a dream that kept recurring frequently, even within one night. He would dream that he was in another city and wanted to phone a certain lady. But the dial on the telephone was so gigantic—it contained some hundred numbers—that he never succeeded in placing the call. After waking, the patient realized that the number he meant to dial was not the lady's but that of a record company for which he was then working with great financial success. As a matter of fact, the patient was a composer of popular music. Now, in the discussion of his dream it turned out that he had actually spent a very satisfying time in the city he dreamed of, composing religious music, whereas his work, although outwardly successful, did not give him inner fulfillment. Except for his composing, he cherished no pleasant memories connected with that city. In particular, he had no longing for that lady, with whom he had never had any erotic relationship. On the other hand, he spontaneously declared that the gigantic dial signified the trouble he had when choosing. (To understand the symbolism of the dream we have to realize that in German the same word, *wählen*, means choosing and dialing.) What then was the patient's choice? It did not refer to a number to dial but rather the vocation to choose—specifically, to the choice between keeping a well-paying, unsatisfying job as a composer of hits and becoming a writer of religious music. Suddenly the essential meaning of the dream became clear. Although in vain, the patient had been struggling to be "connected" again, to be "reconnected." Now we have just to replace *reconnexio* with *religio*, which in Latin means the same, and it is obvious that the dream expressed the patient's desire to find his way back to his true religious and artistic vocation.

This dream, unlike the previous one, does not present a warning to the dreamer but rather expresses a self-reproach. In both cases, however, the dream is an utterance of conscience—in the second case, not only of ethical conscience but also of the artistic conscience—and both dreams are expressions of the spiritual unconscious. In the second case, it was a religious problem that constituted the latent dream content. In the following, the same problem is encountered on a more manifest level:

A patient dreamed his father handed over some saccharine to him, but he refused it with the proud remark that he would rather drink coffee or tea bitter than sweetened with some sort of sugar substitute. The free association went literally as follows: "handed over—tradition; but the tradition I got from my father is our religion." The patient continued to associate, saying that the evening before the dream he had read a magazine article recording a dialogue between an existential philosopher and a theologian. The argument of the existential philosopher seemed very plausible to him, and above all he was impressed by the philosopher's rejection of existentially inauthentic religiosity, in particular where the philosopher refused "to flee into a realm of belief and dream," and then exclaimed, "What sort of a motive is it to want to be happy? What we want is truth." So here also, in his waking life, the patient renounced inauthenticity. The same evening the patient had heard a radio sermon that he felt somehow to be cheap consolation—and somehow "sweetish." It also turned out that at one point in the magazine article the question was asked, "What is it like when the taste [!] for living is lost?" With that in mind, we can understand quite well why the existentially inauthentic religious tradition was associated with the realm of taste, and why the image chosen in the dream was the sugar substitute saccharine, taking the place of the genuine sweetener. This choice of symbols became fully clear when we learned that the patient's good luck piece was a religious icon and that he disguised it from unwanted scrutiny by carrying it in a small wooden box that originally had served as a package for saccharine.

In other dreams expressive of the spiritual unconscious we meet the patient's personal problems pertaining not only to religion in general, but also to religious institutions in particular:

A woman dreamed she went to the Alser Church. To that she associated: "On the way to my psychiatrist I pass the Alser Church, and when I pass it I often think, I am on the way to God—not through the church directly, but through psychotherapy. My way to God goes, so to speak, through the doctor. On my way back from the therapy session, of course, I again pass the Alser Church, and so going to therapy is only a detour to the church." The dream itself continues as follows: "The church seems to be deserted." That the church is deserted signifies that the patient has deserted the church. In fact, she had turned her back on the church. The dream continues: "The church is entirely bombed out; the roof has fallen in, and only the altar remains intact." The inner shock the patient experienced from the war has shaken her spiritually, but has also opened her eyes to the central place, the altar, of religion in life. "The blue heavens shine through here; the air is free." Interpretation: Those inner shocks have freed her eyes to see the celestial. "But above me is still the remainder of the roof, beams that threaten to fall down, and I am afraid of that." Interpretation: The patient is afraid of falling back and of once more being buried in debris. "And I flee into the open, somewhat disappointed." Interpretation: The patient actually had recently gone through disappointments not only with her own affirmation of religion, but also with religious institutions. Complete affirmation of her religion had been hampered by occasional impressions of pettiness and narrowness on the part of some priests and theologians.

It was not surprising that the patient had troubles with institutionalized religion, for she said she had experienced ecstatic mystical states several times. Therefore it was interesting to explore this side of her religious problems and to see how far this aspect of the patient's spiritual unconscious found expression in her dreams:

"I find myself on St. Stephen's Square." (This is the center of Catholic Vienna.) "I stand in front of the main door of St. Stephen's Cathedral, and I see that it is closed." Interpretation: She has no access to Christianity. "In the

Cathedral it is dark, but I know God is there." To this the patient produces as a spontaneous association the following quotation from the Psalms: "Truly, you are a hidden God." The dream continued: "I am searching for the entrance." Interpretation: She is searching for an entrance to Christianity. "It is almost twelve noon." Interpretation: It is high time. "Father N. N. is preaching inside." (Father N. N. was for this patient somehow representative of Christianity.) "Through a small window I can see his head." Interpretation: What he represents goes beyond the small part she sees of him. "I want to get inside." Interpretation: She wants to turn away from his appearance and turn toward the essence. "I am running through narrow passages." The connection between narrowness (*Enge*) and anxiety (*Angst*) is well known; the patient, indeed, is anxiously and impatiently striving to reach her goal: "I have a box of candy with me, with the inscription on it, 'God calls.'" Interpretation: She is called to a religious life, which is the goal toward which she is so impatiently striving, and the way to this goal already contains the sweetness of ecstatic mystical experiences. "I take a candy out of the box and eat it, although I know that it may make me sick." The patient had repeatedly reported that she deliberately exposed herself to the risk of insanity as a potential result of her mystic states, i.e., the risk that they might make her "sick." "I am afraid someone may see the inscription on the candy box; I am ashamed and start to erase the inscription." The patient knew that her "case" was going to be published and so tried everything she could to thwart its publication.

Here we are confronted with a fact that will come to be quite important, namely, that people are sometimes ashamed of their religiousness and try to conceal it. The mistake is often made of confounding such shame with neurotic inhibition. Shame, however, is a perfectly natural attitude. Since Max Scheler's work on this subject, we know that shame has a distinctive protective function in love. Its task is to prevent something from becoming a mere object—an object for onlookers. So we could say the cause of love is served by not being observed. Love flees publicness, for man is afraid that what is sacred to him might be profaned by becoming public. More specifically, this profanation might occur through a loss of immediacy in giving oneself to, and loving, the other. Such immediacy, however, is threatened not only by becoming an object for others, but by becoming an object for one's own self-observation as well. In both cases the immediate, original genuineness of love is liable to vanish; its existentiality is liable to dwindle into mere facticity. Being is turned into being observed, be it by oneself, be it by others. Loving is in danger of being "de-self-ified" and "id-ified."

Now, something analogous may happen to religiousness. The quality of intimacy so characteristic of love is no less characteristic of religion. It is intimate in two senses: it is *intimum* in the sense of innermost, and second, it is, like love, protected by shame. Genuine religiousness, for the sake of its own genuineness, hides from the public. That is why religious patients often do not want to deliver their intimate experiences into the hands of people who would perhaps lack understanding and thus misinterpret them. Such patients may be afraid that a psychiatrist will try to "unmask" their religiousness as "nothing but" the manifestation of unconscious psychodynamics, of conflicts or complexes. Or they may fear just as much that their religiousness will be interpreted as something impersonal—be it in the sense of unconscious "archetypes" or of the "collective unconscious."

One can understand why the patient shied away from seeing herself one day published as a "case," and her religious feelings thereby somehow debased into the mere object of a detached scientific investigation. Of course, patients are reluctant not only to become "cases" in publications, but also to be "demonstrated" before a public—such as being part of clinical demonstrations of psychotherapy to medical students. In the classroom setting we could witness time and again that patients who are quite ready to talk about their sexual lives in the most intimate and even perverse details are the same ones who display marked inhibitions as soon as the discussion turns to their intimate religious life.

For example, during one of these demonstrations a patient happened to be asked if she could reproduce a dream, and she came up with the following one: "I am in the middle of a great crowd of people; it is like a fair. Everyone is moving in one direction, while I myself try to go in the opposite direction." Interpretation: In the "fair" that this world is, the great masses of people are all alike. The patient, however, is swimming against the current. "Somehow I know the direction in which I have to go, for from the heavens shines a light which I am going toward. This light gets brighter and brighter and finally condenses into a figure." Interpretation: At first the patient knew the direction only approximately, but now she knows it more precisely. Then we asked what sort of a figure it was. With that, however, the patient became embarrassed, and after much hesitation she asked with an imploring look, "Do I really have to talk about that?" Only after much persuasion did she let out her secret and murmur, "The figure was Christ." In her dream her conscience had demanded that she follow Christ.

In this dream there is scarcely any religious problem left, since to this patient it was unquestionable that she had to take the religious path. In contrast, the dreams reported before this one showed clear-cut religious problems, be they manifest or latent, depending on whether the religiousness was conscious to the patient or had been repressed by him into the unconscious. That repression of religiousness can occur is no longer a surprise when we

realize the intimate quality inherent in genuine religiousness. Nor is it surprising occasionally to find flagrantly
religious motifs in dreams of people who are manifestly
irreligious, because we have seen that there is not only
repressed and unconscious *libido*, but also repressed and
unconscious *religio*.

One of my patients once spontaneously declared:
"How come I am ashamed of whatever is religious, that it
seems to me bothersome and ridiculous? Well, I know very
well myself why I feel so ashamed about my religious
longings: Underlying all the psychotherapeutic treatment
I have had these last 27 years was the more or less tacit
conviction on the part of my doctors that such longings
are nothing but unrealistic, baseless speculation. As they
put it, only the tangible is real, and everything else is
nonsense, caused by a trauma or by the wish to escape life
by fleeing into disease. So whenever I expressed my
longing for God I was almost afraid they would bring in
the straitjacket. Until now every type of psychotherapy
missed the point."

A patient of mine wanted to discover why she had
such a dislike for Christianity. She had not practiced her
religion since childhood. In a deliberate combination of
logotherapy and suggestive measures I gave her the post
hypnotic suggestion, "Tonight I shall receive the answer
from my dreams." This is the dream that she reported the
next day:

"I am in the town where I spent my childhood. I am
waiting for a train to Vienna." The patient thereby sums
up her way from the past into the present. "Dr. X lives
there. I want to visit him." Dr. X is a well-known
psychotherapist and a good friend of the patient's family.
Thus the dream indicates a need for psychotherapy. "I
don't know what Dr. X's address is. I ask a woman and
she says, 'Near the church.'" The patient knows that her
recovery in psychotherapy can only be completed through

religion. "I am thinking in the dream, eventually I shall find the church again." So she is optimistic. Needless to say, the "church" here means more than just the building. Thus the dream indicates her hope and conviction that she will find her way back to religion. "But everything is different from what it used to be." To find this way back is not so simple for an adult who has been chased through the hell of life and of doubt. "I wonder which street to take." Which way should she take to come back to religion? "I have been walking a long time. I feel doubtful." In the dream this doubt refers to the way to Dr. X, but in reality it is doubt about God. "A little girl is standing in front of me and gives me information." Spontaneously the patient observed that this girl represented herself as she was in her childhood. So I asked her whether she knew the biblical saying, "You must become like children again," and the patient told me that this passage had always impressed her deeply. And what was the information this girl handed out in the dream? "Near the church; but you have taken the wrong way—you must go back." So the patient feels that first she must go back to the simplicity of children as this characterizes their faith. "I am thirsty." To this the patient associates a verse from the Psalms: "As the hart panteth after the water brooks, so panteth my soul after thee. . . ." The dream continues: "The child draws clear water from a spring, and now I am actually going back." The way back means psychotherapy—more specifically, existential analysis. "Suddenly I see poplars lying across the street." These fallen poplars signify the difficulties and relapses that had emerged during therapy. "But then the way is clear, again, and in the distance is the church—a miraculous cathedral, milky white, like the one in Caen." In her own attempt to interpret the dream it came out that, when driving to France on a trip some years before, she had looked forward to seeing the cathedral because she had known it from pictures and admired it very much. But when her party arrived in Caen it was so dark and so foggy that she never actually saw the cathedral. We feel justified in interpreting the transformation of the cathedral, which she had never seen but had so much longed for, into the splendorous sight of the church in the dream, as a symbol of the transformation of the patient's concept of God that had taken place through treatment—namely, the transition from the *Deus absconditus* into the *Deus revelatus*.

CHAPTER 5

The Transcendent Quality of Conscience

In the existential analysis of dreams in the preceding chapter, the psychological fact of repressed and unconscious religiousness became obvious. And the empirical results of existential analysis came up to its ontological expectations. In fact, if the existential analysis of conscience is carried further, one will be confronted with a very significant finding, which may best be described as the transcendent quality of conscience. To illuminate this finding, start with the following assumptions:

All freedom has a "from what" and a "to what." The "from what" of man's freedom is his being driven, and the "to what" is his being responsible, his having conscience. These two facets of the human condition are best expressed by a simple admonition from Maria von Ebner-Eschenbach: "Be the master of your will and the servant of your conscience!" From this sentence, from this moral imperative, we would like to start to illuminate what we have called the transcendent quality of conscience.

"Be the master of your will . . ." Well, I am already the master of my will insofar as I am human and fully aware of my humanness—that is to say, insofar as I am interpreting this humanness in terms of responsibleness.

But if I am also to be "the servant of my conscience," then I may ask whether this conscience has not to be something other than I myself; might it not be something higher than he who merely perceives its "voice?" In other words, I cannot be the servant of my conscience unless I understand conscience as a phenomenon transcendent of man. So I cannot consider conscience simply in terms of its psychological facticity, but must also grasp it in its transcendent essence. I can be the servant of my conscience only when the dialogue with my conscience is a genuine *dia-logos* rather than a mere *mono-logos*. This, however, can only be so when my conscience transcends my self, when it is the mediator of something other than my self.

It would seem, therefore, that the phrase "the voice of conscience," common to so many languages, is based on a mistake. If conscience "had" a voice it could not "be" a voice itself—the voice of transcendence. Then man would not only overhear this voice—it would stem from him. But only the transcendent quality of conscience makes it possible to understand man in depth or, more specifically, to understand his being a person. The very term "person," seen in this light, takes on a new meaning, for now one may say: Through the conscience of the human person, a transhuman agent *per-sonat*—which literally means, "is sounding through." It is not up to us to answer the question of what this "agent" is, since our concern with the origin of conscience is anthropological rather than theological. Nonetheless we may be justified in claiming that this transhuman agent must necessarily be of a personal nature. More correctly, however, we would have to speak of a transpersonal agent of which the human person is but the "image."

So conscience is not only a fact within psychological immanence but also a referent to transcendence; only with reference to transcendence, only as some sort of transcendent phenomenon, can it really be understood. It is like the human navel, which would appear meaningless if it were taken as an isolated phenomenon; the navel can only be understood in the context of the prenatal history, for it points beyond the individual to his origin in his mother. It is the same with conscience; it can only be fully understood as a phenomenon pointing to its own transcendent origin. As long as we consider man as an isolated being without the context of his origin, some things about him must elude our understanding; and what holds for the ontogenesis of man also is true of ontology. We cannot ontologically understand such a human phenomenon as conscience unless we reach back to its transcendent origin. Conscience is fully understandable only against the background of a transhuman dimension. To explain man's being free, the existential quality of the human reality would do; however, to explain his being responsible, the transcendent quality of conscience must be considered.

So conscience, which we have taken as our model of the spiritual unconscious, is seen to have a key position in disclosing to us the essential transcendence of the spiritual unconscious. The psychological fact of conscience is but the immanent aspect of a transcendent phenomenon; it is only that piece of the whole phenomenon that seeps into psychological immanence.

If conscience is the voice of transcendence it is thus itself transcendent. Viewed in this light, an irreligious man is one who does not recognize this transcendent quality. Needless to say, the irreligious man also "has" a conscience, and he also is responsible; he simply asks no further— neither what he is responsible to, nor from what his conscience stems. But this is no reason for the religious man to become haughty. Consider the biblical story of Samuel: When Samuel was a boy he once spent a night in the Temple with the high priest Eli. He was awakened by a voice calling him by name. He rose and asked Eli what he wanted, but the high priest had not called him and told him to go back to sleep. The same thing happened a second time, and only when it happened a third time did the high priest tell the boy that the next time he heard his name called, he should stand up and say, "Speak, Lord; for thy servant heareth."

If Samuel failed to recognize that the call came to him from transcendence, how much more difficult it must be for an ordinary person to discern the transcendent character of the voice he perceives through his conscience. And why should we be surprised if he takes this voice for something that is rooted merely within himself?

The irreligious man thus proves to be the one who takes his conscience in its psychological facticity. Facing it as merely an immanent fact, he stops—stops prematurely—for he considers conscience the ultimate "to what" he is responsible. However, conscience is not the last "to what" of responsibleness, but the next to last. On his way to find the ultimate meaning of life, the irreligious man, as it were, has not yet reached the highest peak, but rather has stopped at the next to highest. (This, of course, is the way the *religious* man looks at the irreligious.) And what is the reason the irreligious man does not go further? It is because he does not want to lose the "firm ground under his feet." The true summit is barred from his vision; it is hidden in the fog, and he does not risk venturing into it, into this uncertainty. Only the religious man hazards it.

The more religious a man is, the more he will respect the decision of his fellow man not to go further. After all, it is precisely the religious man who should respect the freedom of such a choice, because he is the one who believes man to be created free. And this freedom includes the possibility of saying no, for instance, by deliberately refusing to accept any religious *Weltanschauung*. To be sure, among those who have committed themselves to an atheistic or agnostic worldview, there are some who are ready to accept the concept of transcendence, but do not feel that this necessitates that they speak of "God." However, there are others who do not see any reason why not to denote transcendence by the age-old word "God."

Conscience not only refers to transcendence; it also originates in transcendence. This fact accounts for its irreducible quality. Therefore, if we raise the question of the origin of conscience, there can be no psychological answer but only an ontological one. Any attempt at a mere ontic reduction, any attempt to reduce conscience to psychodynamics, proves futile. This was clearly seen by the nineteenth-century writer Hebbel when; he wrote in a letter of May 13, 1857, addressed to Uechtritz: "Conscience stands in striking contrast to any values that might be put forward by materialism. If one tries to reduce conscience to the sexual drive or to the instinct of propagation—something that surely will happen sooner or later, if it has not already happened—even then conscience will be neither explained away nor done away with." What Hebbel prophesied here has in the meantime happened. Indeed, psychoanalysis has tried to explain conscience in psychodynamic terms, reducing it to the superego and deducing the superego from the introjected father image.

However, just as the self cannot be identified with the ego, likewise conscience cannot be identified with the superego. Rather, one must acknowledge the irreducibility of these two phenomena: the existential quality of the self and the transcendent quality of conscience. As to the first phenomenon, man's being responsible can never be traced back to his being driven—the self can never be traced back to any drives or instincts. The self has the function of repressing and sublimating the drives and instincts but can itself never be derived from them. Even if instinctual energy is utilized in repression and sublimation, that which puts this energy into motion cannot itself be explained merely in terms of instinctual energy. Has anyone seen a river building its own power plant? It was man who dammed the water to utilize its energy.

But just as drives and instincts cannot repress themselves, likewise the self cannot be responsible merely to itself. The self cannot be its own lawgiver. It can never issue any autonomous "categorical imperative," for a categorical imperative can receive its credentials only from transcendence. Its categorical character stands and falls with its transcendent quality. It is true that man is responsible for himself, but ultimately he is not responsible before himself. Not only man's being free, but also his being responsible requires an intentional referent. Just as freedom means little, indeed nothing, without a "to what," so responsibleness is incomplete without a "to what."

Goethe once said: *"Alles Wollen ist ja nur ein Wollen, weil wir eben sollten"*—whenever man wills, this act of will always presupposes a grasp of what he ought to do. The "ought" is ontologically prior to the will. Just as I can only answer if I am first questioned, just as each reply requires a "to what," and such a "to what" must be prior to the reply itself, so the "to what" of all responsibleness must necessarily be prior to responsibleness itself.

What I feel that I ought to do, or ought to be, could never be effective if it were nothing but an invention of mine—rather than a discovery. Jean Paul Sartre believed that man can choose and design himself by creating his own standards. However, to ascribe to the self such a creative power seems to be still within the old idealistic tradition. Is it not even comparable to the fakir trick? The fakir claims to throw a rope into the air, into the empty space, and claims a boy will climb up the rope. It is not different with Sartre when he tries to make us believe that man "projects" himself—throws himself forward and upward—into nothingness.

It may be said that the psychoanalytic superego theory comes down to the contention that the ego pulls itself up by the bootstraps of the superego out of the bog of the id. However, the superego is not the only thing regarded as an (introjected) father image; the God concept too is interpreted in terms of a (projected) father image. Now let us for heuristic purposes play off the psycho-analytic view against the theological. A Copernican switch would be the result. For theology God is not a father image, but rather the father is an image of God. In this view the father is not the model of divinity, but on the contrary, God is the model of paternity. Biographically and biologically the father is first; theologically, however, God is first. Psychologically the relationship between the child and his father is prior to the relationship between man and God; theologically, however, my natural father, and in this sense my creator, is but the first representative of a supernatural father and creator of the universe.

Many psychoanalysts have interpreted all religion merely in terms of sublimation and thus have reduced all religious experience, be it conscious or unconscious and repressed, to infantile sexuality. To this one might say: No one will be able to make us believe that man is a sublimated animal once we can show that within him there is a repressed angel.

CHAPTER 6

Unconscious Religiousness

By examining the results attained in the previous five chapters together with results previously obtained by existential analysis, it can be seen that the approach has been developed in three main stages:

The starting point was the basic phenomenological fact that being human is being conscious and being responsible, culminating in a synthesis of both—namely, in one's consciousness of his responsibleness.[1]

The second stage of development was reached when existential analysis ventured into unconscious spirituality. In 1926, logotherapy—the clinical application of our existential analytic approach—had extended the scope of psychotherapy beyond the *psyche*, beyond the psychological dimension to include the noölogical dimension, or the *logos*; in the second stage, the *unconscious* logos was disclosed with the discovery of a spiritual unconscious in addition to the instinctual unconscious. In these unconscious spiritual depths the great existential choices are made. It follows, then, that man's being responsible reaches down into an unconscious ground; thus, besides conscious responsibleness there must also be unconscious responsibleness.

With the discovery of the spiritual unconscious, existential analysis eluded the peril to which psychoanalysis had succumbed, namely, of id-ifying the unconscious. With the concept of the spiritual unconscious, existential analytical logotherapy also avoided any one-sided intellectualism and rationalism in its theory of man. Logos is deeper than logic. Thus the fact that man can no longer be considered as a totally rational being has been recognized by logotherapy without falling prey to the *other* extreme, i.e., idolizing the irrational and the instinctual, as did psychoanalysis.

Now, in its third stage of development, existential analysis has uncovered—within the spiritual unconscious—unconscious religiousness. This unconscious religiousness, revealed by our phenomenological analysis, is to be understood as a latent relation to transcendence inherent in man. If one prefers, one might conceive of this relation in terms of a relationship between the immanent self and a transcendent Thou. However one wishes to formulate it, we are confronted with what I should like to term "the transcendent unconscious" as part and parcel of the spiritual unconscious. This concept means no more or less than that man has always stood in an intentional relation to transcendence, even if only on an unconscious level. If one calls the intentional referent of such an unconscious relation "God," it is apt to speak of an "unconscious God." This, however, in no way implies that God is unconscious to himself, but rather that God may be unconscious to man and that man's relation to God may be unconscious.

In the Psalms mention is made of "the hidden God," and Hellenistic culture dedicated an altar to "the unknown God." Similarly, our concept of an unconscious God refers to man's hidden relation to a God who himself is hidden.

The phrase "unconscious God" could be misinterpreted in three ways. First of all, it could be misunderstood as pantheistic. It would be a complete misconception to assume that the unconscious is itself divine. It is only related to the divine. That man has an unconscious relation to God does not at all mean that God is "within us," that he "inhabits" our unconscious—all this is but a notion of theological dilettantism.

Another potential misinterpretation of the unconscious God concept would be to take it in the sense of occultism. The paradox of an "unconscious knowledge" of God would be mistakenly interpreted to mean that the unconscious is omniscient, or even knows better than the conscious self. Not only is the unconscious not divine, but furthermore, it does not possess any attribute of the divine, and thus lacks divine omniscience as well. As the first misinterpretation had to be rejected as theological dilettantism, the second one amounts to instant metaphysics.

No knowledge can come to know itself, to judge itself, without rising above itself. In the same vein, no science can weigh its own results and realize their implications without transcending its own ontic sphere and subjecting itself to ontological scrutiny. That is the reason that compelled us to go beyond the borders of strict science in order to see how the result of our phenomenological, and in this sense empirical, investigation matched up with the ontological expectations. This makes it even more important to keep the firm ground of empirical and clinical data under our feet lest we fall into what we denoted as theological dilettantism and instant metaphysics. Our task is to start with simple experiential facts and to evaluate them along the lines of traditional psychiatric methodology—for example, by invoking the classical method of free association in our dream analyses. To be sure, while so doing we paid due tribute to phenomenological "facts" as well. These facts, too, are "factual," and they are so to the extent that they do not allow for any further analytical reduction. Consider the flagrantly religious dreams of what were known to be manifestly irreligious patients. What is most striking in such dreams is an ecstatic experience of bliss that was unknown to the patient in his waking life. It is simply impossible to insist that behind such an experience there must be a sexual meaning—unless we choose to violate our intellectual honesty by pressing phenomena into the Procrustean bed—not to say, the Procrustean couch—of preconceived patterns of interpretation.

And now to the third and most important potential misinterpretation: It cannot be emphasized strongly enough that not only is the unconscious neither divine nor omniscient, but above all man's unconscious relation to God is profoundly personal. The "unconscious God" must not be mistaken as an impersonal force operant in man. This misunderstanding was the great mistake to which C. G. Jung fell prey. Jung must be credited with having discovered distinctly religious elements within the unconscious. Yet he misplaced this unconscious religiousness of man, failing to locate the unconscious God in the personal and existential region. Instead, he allotted it to the region of drives and instincts, where unconscious religiousness no longer remained a matter of choice and decision. According to Jung, something within me is religious, but it is not I who then is religious; something within me drives me to God, but it is not I who makes the choice and takes the responsibility.

For Jung, unconscious religiousness was bound up with religious archetypes belonging to the collective unconscious. For him, unconscious religiousness has scarcely anything to do with a personal decision, but becomes an essentially impersonal, collective, "typical" (i.e., archetypical) process occurring in man. However, it is our contention that religiousness could emerge least of all from a collective unconscious, precisely because religion involves the most personal decisions man makes, even if only on an unconscious level. But there is no possibility of leaving such decisions to some processes merely taking place in me.

For Jung and the Jungians unconscious religiousness has always remained something more or less instinctual. H. Bänziger, in a paper published in 1947 in the *Schweizerische Zeitschrift für Psychologie,* even bluntly declares: "We may speak of a *religious drive* just as we speak of sexual and aggressive drives" (the italics are Bänziger's!). But what sort of religion would that be—a religion to which I am driven, driven just as I am driven to sex? As for myself, I would not give a damn for a religiousness that I owed to some "religious drive." Genuine religiousness has not the character of drivenness but rather that of deciding-ness. Indeed, religiousness stands with its deciding-ness—and falls with its drivenness. In a word, religiousness is either existential or not at all.

For Jung, however—and in this respect he does not really differ from Freud—the unconscious, including its religious aspects, is something that determines the person. In contrast, we contend that the religious unconscious, or for that matter the spiritual unconscious, is a *deciding* being-unconscious rather than a being driven by the unconscious. As we see it, the spiritual unconscious and, even more, its religious aspects—that is to say, what we have called the transcendent unconscious—is an existential agent rather than an instinctual factor. As such it belongs to spiritual existence rather than psychophysical facticity. This, however, was completely neglected by Jung when he wrote that archetypes should be understood as "a structural property or condition characteristic of the psyche which is in some way connected with the brain."[2] Thereby religiousness becomes entirely a matter of the somatic and psychic conditions of human existence—while it is really a matter of the spiritual person who builds on those conditions.

As Jung saw it, the religious archetypes are impersonal forms of the collective unconscious that can be unearthed as more or less preformed psychological facts, and as such pertain to psychophysical facticity. From this region they operate as autonomous powers—autonomous in the sense that they are independent of personal decisions. Our point of view, however, is that unconscious religiousness stems from the personal center of the individual man rather than an impersonal pool of images shared by mankind.

If we respect the spiritual and existential character of unconscious religiousness—rather than allotting it to the realm of psychological facticity—it also becomes impossible to regard it as something innate. Since it is not tied up with heredity in the biological sense, it cannot be inherited either. This is not to deny that all religiousness always proceeds within certain preestablished paths and patterns of development. These, however, are not innate, inherited archetypes but given cultural molds into which personal religiousness is poured. These molds are not transmitted in a biological way, but are passed down through the world of traditional symbols indigenous to a given culture. This world of symbols is not inborn in us, but we are born into it.

Thus there are religious forms, and they wait to be assimilated by man in an existential way, i.e., to be made his own. But what serves this purpose is not any archetype, but rather the prayers[3] of our fathers, the rites of our churches and synagogues,[4] the revelations of our prophets and the examples set by saints and zaddiks. Culture offers enough traditional molds for man to fill with lived religion; no one has to invent God. On the other hand, no one carries him along in the form of an innate archetype.

Primary religiousness therefore must not simply be identified with primitive or archaic religiousness. However, it is true time and again that primary religiousness that has fallen prey to repression comes to the surface in the form of a naïve or childlike faith. But nothing else should be expected, for such religiousness necessarily is associated with experiential material accrued during childhood. In fact, whenever an existential analysis unearths this material and releases it from repression, we are confronted with a faith that indeed is childlike in the truest, best sense of the word. No matter how childlike and naïve it may be, it is in no way primitive, nor is it archaic in the sense of Jung's archetypes. If one embarks on an unbiased analysis, he will not be confronted with elements of a pseudoarchaic mythology, but rather with religious experiences engraved in memories from one's childhood.

Existential analysis has moved even further beyond Freud's view of religion. It is no longer necessary to ponder "the future of an illusion," but our thoughts do revolve around the apparent timelessness of a reality— around the ever-present reality that man's intrinsic religiousness has revealed itself to be. It is a reality in the strict sense of phenomenological empiricism. To be sure, it also is a reality that can remain, or again become, unconscious, or be repressed. Precisely in such cases, however, it is the task of logotherapy to remind the patient of his unconscious religiousness—that is to say, to let it enter his conscious mind again. After all, it is the business of existential analytic logotherapy to trace the neurotic mode of being to its ultimate ground. Sometimes the ground of neurotic existence is to be seen in a deficiency, in that a person's relation to transcendence is repressed. But although concealed in "the transcendent unconscious," repressed transcendence shows up and makes itself noticeable as an "unrest of the heart." In my book *The Doctor and the Soul* I described a case in which this restlessness precipitated a "psychosomatic," or really noösomatic, heart condition. So what holds for the unconscious in general is also true of unconscious religiousness in particular: Repression winds up in neurosis.

There is clinical evidence for this assertion. Take the example of a patient suffering from a severe obsessive-compulsive neurosis that for decades had defied long-term treatment by various psychoanalysts. The symp-tomatological picture was dominated by the obsessive fear that whatever he did might eventuate in the eternal damnation of his late mother or sister. For this reason the patient would not accept a government position, for he would have had to take an oath of office, which at some later time he might have violated, if only in a trifling way. In consequence, mother and sister would be damned. The patient had also evaded marriage, simply because he would have had to say "I do" at the wedding, and if he were ever somehow to go against his marriage vows, that could also have led to the damnation of his dead mother and sister. He had not bought a radio just because, in the moment he was going to buy it, the obsessive thought went through his head that if he did not immediately grasp a certain technical detail his mother and sister would have to face a terrible fate in hell.

Confronted with such an abundance of more or less religious references in the patient's account, we asked him what his attitude was toward religion. To our surprise, it turned out that he considered himself a full-fledged "freethinker." More specifically, he declared himself to be a follower of Haeckel (a popularizer of a biologically oriented materialism well known around the turn of the century). And with obvious pride he related how much his understanding of modern physics had advanced through private studies; for example, he had completely mastered the theory of the electron. To the question whether he knew anything about religious matters, he indeed admitted that he knew the prayer book but only "as the criminal knows the code of law." By this he meant that he was aware of it but did not care for it. To the question whether, then, he was irreligious, he responded, "Who can say that of himself? Sure, I am irreligious intellectually, but emotionally I still might believe. Intellectually I believe only in natural laws—not in anything such as a God who rewards and punishes." And behold, the same individual who uttered these words had shortly before, when reporting on his sexual impotence, remarked, "At that moment I was haunted by the obsessive idea that God could take revenge on me."

Freud, in *The Future of an Illusion,* said, "Religion is the universal compulsive neurosis of mankind; like that of the child, it derives from the Oedipal complex, from the relationship to the father." In view of the case history abstracted above, we are tempted to reverse Freud's statement and dare to say compulsive neurosis may well be diseased religiousness. In fact, clinical evidence suggests that atrophy of the religious sense in man results in a distortion of his religious concepts. Or, to put it in a less clinical vein, once the angel in us is repressed, he turns into a demon. There is even a parallel on the sociocultural level, for time and again we watch and witness how repressed religion degenerates into superstition. In our century, a deified reason and a megalomanic technology are the repressive structures to which the religious feeling is sacrificed. This fact explains much of the present condition of man, which indeed resembles a "universal compulsive neurosis of mankind," to quote Freud. Much of man's present condition? Yes—with one exception: religion.

With special reference to technology, however, one is reminded of a dictum by Goethe: "He who possesses art and science also has religion." But today we know only too well where man would wind up if he had science and nothing beyond it: Soon the only thing that would be left of all his science would be the atom bombs he possessed.

But let us turn away from problems of humanity and return to the compulsive neurosis of the individual. In concluding this chapter we might venture to say that God is a "vengeful God" indeed, for neurotic existence in some cases seems to be the toll that a crippled relation to transcendence takes on man.

CHAPTER 7

Psychotherapy and Theology

We may well ask what bearing all the questions raised so far might have on research and practice in the field of psychiatry. After all, it is not for the medical profession to be interested in theological problems. When such matters come into discussion, the physician is bound to unconditional tolerance. Least of all is a physician who personally is religious released from this obligation. He will only be interested in a spontaneous breakthrough of religiousness on the part of the patient. And he will be patient enough to wait for such a spontaneous development to take place. This should not be difficult for him since precisely he, as a religious person, is convinced that even in a manifestly irreligious person there must be latent religiousness. After all, the religious psychiatrist believes not only in God, but also in an unconscious belief on the part of the patient. In other words, he believes that his own God is "the unconscious God" of the patient. And, at the same time, he believes that this unconscious God is one who has simply *not yet* become conscious to the patient.

We have said that religion is genuine only where it is existential, where man is not somehow driven to it, but commits himself to it by freely choosing to be religious. Now we have seen that the existentiality of religiousness has to be matched by its spontaneity. Genuine religiousness must unfold in its own time. Never can anyone be forced to it. So we may say, to genuine religiousness man cannot be driven by an instinct—nor pushed by a psychiatrist.

As Freud has taught us, the process by which unconscious material becomes conscious has a therapeutic effect only if the process takes place spontaneously. The working through of repressed material is based on its spontaneously breaking through, and I think that something analogous also holds for repressed religiousness. Here, to exert any pressure along the lines of a preestablished program would be self-defeating; in this case, intention would thwart the effect. This is a fact of which even the clergy is quite aware. Even the clergy would insist on the full spontaneity of true religiousness; all the more should a psychiatrist. I well remember, for example, how a priest described being called to the deathbed of a man whom he knew to be irreligious. The man had simply felt the need to speak out his mind before he died, and had for this purpose chosen the priest. The priest told me that he had refrained from offering the last rites to the man for the simple reason that he had not spontaneously asked for them. So great was the priest's own insistence on spontaneity!

But should we psychiatrists be more priestly than the priests? Should we not instead have at least as much respect as this priest had for the free decisions of our patients, particularly in religious matters?

But time and again psychotherapists try to outdo even the priests. This is just hubris. The function of the psychiatrist cannot be distinguished sharply enough from the mission of the clergy. Just as the irreligious psychiatrist should let the religious patient have his belief, likewise the religious psychiatrist must let the priest keep his priestly office.

Elsewhere we have shown that it is characteristic of obsessive-compulsive patients to be dominated by a

Faustian will that everything be "100 percent," that absolute certainty be reached in their acts of cognition and decision. As it were, they are hung up on the promise of the serpent: *Eritis sicut Deus, scientem bonum et malum* (You will be like God, knowing what is good and what is evil). And of those psychotherapists who try to usurp the duties of the clergy, we may say that they wish *esse sicut pastores, demonstrantes bonum et malum*—they wish to be, not like God, but like the priests, not knowing, but showing what is good and what is evil.

We have often said that logotherapy is not meant to substitute for psychotherapy but, rather, to supplement it. Likewise we have often pointed out that what we call medical ministry is in no way supposed to replace the pastoral ministry. This, however, does not do away with the possibility that the psychiatrist, if need be, may take over the function of the priest. The following is an instance of how this can happen:

An old woman came to the psychotherapeutic outpatient clinic of our department to consult us on her severe depression. She had no family left since her daughter, her only child, had recently committed suicide. She could not get over that. After her mourning showed itself to be not pathological but a normal reaction, the psychiatrist cautiously asked her how she felt about religion. Since the patient said she was religious, he inquired why, then, she had not instead sought the help of a priest. She replied that she had gone to her priest, but he had not had even a few minutes for her. However, the psychiatrist, himself a religious man, could easily give this woman the consolation she needed—that consolation on the grounds of their common faith that her priest had not been able to provide. The situation required that the psychiatrist take the place of the priest in order to give religious comfort. This was not only his human right, but even his religious duty, for in this case one religious person was confronting another. What we wish to stress, however, is that the psychiatrist is never entitled to such a religious approach *qua* psychiatrist, but only as a religious person. Furthermore, only a psychiatrist who is himself a religious person is justified in bringing religion into psychotherapy. An irreligious psychiatrist never has the right to manipulate the patient's religious feelings by employing religion as just another useful tool to try—along with such things as pills, shots, and shocks. This would be to debase religion and degrade it to a mere device for improving mental health.

Although religion might have a very positive psycho-therapeutic effect on the patient, its intention is in no way a psychotherapeutic one. Although religion might secondarily promote such things as mental health and inner equilibrium, its aim does not primarily concern psycho-logical solutions but, rather, spiritual salvation. Religion is not an insurance policy for a tranquil life, for maximum freedom from conflicts, or for any other hygienic goal. Religion provides man with more than psychotherapy ever could—but it also demands more of him. Any fusion of the respective goals of religion and psychotherapy must result in con-fusion. The fact remains that the intentions of the two are different—even if their effects might overlap. In the same vein, any attempt to merge the medical ministry with the pastoral one is to be rejected. There are some authors who propose that psychotherapy relinquish its autonomy as a science and its independence from religion in favor of seeing its function as that of an *ancilla theologiae*. As is well known, for centuries philosophy was allotted the role of such an *ancilla theologiae*, i.e., a handmaid in the service of theology.

However, just as the dignity of man is based on his freedom—to the extent that he may even say no to God—so the dignity of a science is based on that unconditional freedom that guarantees its independent search for truth.

And just as human freedom must include the freedom to say no, so the freedom of scientific investigation must face the risk that its results will turn out to contradict religious beliefs and convictions. Only a scientist who is ready to fight militantly for such an autonomy of thought may triumphantly live to see how the results of his research eventually fit, without contradictions, in the truths of his belief.

Speaking of dignity—be it the dignity of man or that of science—we may define it as the value of something *in itself*, as opposed to its value *for me*. Thus we could say that whoever tries to make psychotherapy into an *ancilla theologiae*, a servant to theology, not only robs it of the dignity of an autonomous science but also takes away the potential value it might have for religion, because psychotherapy can be useful to religion only in terms of a by-product, or a side effect, and never if its usefulness is intended from the start. If psychotherapy is ever to serve religion—either by the results of its empirical investigation or by the therapeutic effects of treatment—psychotherapy has to refrain from setting any preconceived goals along religious lines. Only those results that have been obtained by independent research, uninfluenced by presuppositions borrowed from religion, can ever be of use and value for theology. And if psychotherapy is ever to offer evidence that the human psyche really is what we think it is, namely, *anima naturaliter religiosa* (religious by nature), such evidence can only be offered by a psychotherapy that is *scientia naturaliter irreligiosa*—that is to say, a psychotherapy that by its very nature is not and can never be religiously oriented.

The less psychotherapy condescends to serve theology as a handmaid, the greater will be the service it actually performs.

One need not be a servant to be able to serve.

CHAPTER 8

New Research in Logotherapy circa 1975

In the preface to the first English edition of *The Unconscious God* (1975), I promised to examine some of the tenets that, since the first publication in German in 1947, have been further elaborated. Understandably, I will have to concentrate on conscience as one of the most important phenomena central to these tenets. According to the logotherapeutic theory, conscience has a very specific function. However, in order to fully clarify this function, I must first chart the motivation theory as it underlies logotherapy.

According to most of the current motivation theories, man is a being basically concerned with gratifying needs and satisfying drives and instincts; he does so, in the final analysis, only to alleviate the inner tension created by them, to the end of maintaining, or restoring, an inner equilibrium called "homeostasis." This is a concept originally borrowed from biology but that was eventually found even there to be untenable. Ludwig von Bertalanffy had long maintained and demonstrated that primordial biological phenomena such as growth and reproduction cannot be explained along the lines of the homeostasis principle. Kurt Goldstein even proved that only a brain that is functioning pathologically is characterized by the attempt to avoid tension unconditionally. I for one think that man is never primarily concerned with any inner condition, such as the inner equilibrium, but rather with something or someone out there in the world, be it a cause to serve or a partner to love—and if he really loves the partner, he certainly does not just use him as a more or less apt means to satisfying his own needs.

Thus, human existence—at least as long as it has not been neurotically distorted—is always directed to something, or someone, other than itself, be it a meaning to fulfill or another human being to encounter lovingly. I have termed this constitutive characteristic of human existence "self-transcendence."[1] What is called "self-actualization" is ultimately an effect, the unintentional by-product, of self-transcendence. So it turns out that Pindar's imperative that one should become what one is—in other words, that man should actualize his potentialities—is valid only if we add what Karl Jaspers once said: "What one is, he has become through that cause which he has made his own." Or, as Abraham H. Maslow put it, the "business of self-actualization" can best be carried out "via a commitment to an important job."[2]

Just as self-actualization can be obtained only through a detour, through the fulfillment of meaning, so identity is available only through responsibility, through being responsible for the fulfillment of meaning. It is fitting that research conducted at Boston University, based on a new test that "measures the collective neurosis as formulated by logotherapy," shows that there "appears to be a negative correlation between the collective neurosis and responsibility."[3]

Therefore man is originally characterized by his "search for meaning" rather than his "search for himself." The more he forgets himself—giving himself to a cause or another person—the more *human* he is. And the more he is immersed and absorbed in something or someone other than himself the more he really becomes *himself*. Just consider a child who, absorbed in play, forgets himself—this is the moment to take a snapshot; when you wait until he notices that you are taking a picture, his face congeals and freezes, showing his unnatural self-consciousness rather than his natural graciousness. Why do most people have that stereotyped expression on their faces whenever they are photographed? This expression stems from their concern with the impression they are going to leave on the onlooker. It is "cheese" that makes them so ugly. Forgetting themselves, the photographer, and the future onlooker would make them beautiful.

Consider the eye. The eye, too, is self-transcendent in a way. The moment it perceives something of itself, its function—to perceive the surrounding world visually— has deteriorated. If it is afflicted with a cataract, it may "perceive" its own cataract as a cloud; and if it is suffering from glaucoma, it might "see" its own glaucoma as a rainbow halo around lights. Normally, however, the eye doesn't see anything of itself. Equally, by virtue of the self-transcendent quality of the human reality, the humanness of man is most tangible when he forgets himself—and overlooks himself!

One of the two aspects of self-transcendence, namely, reaching out for a meaning to fulfill, is identical with what I have come to call "the will to meaning." This concept, which occupies such a central place in the motivation theory of logotherapy, denotes the fundamental fact that normally—or in neurotic cases, originally—man is striving to find, and fulfill, meaning and purpose in life. This concept of a will to meaning has been empirically corroborated and validated by several authors, who based their research on tests and statistics. James C. Crumbaugh and Leonard T. Maholick's Purpose-in-Life-Test (PIL)[4] and Elisabeth S. Lukas's Logo-Test were given to thousands of subjects, and after the data had been computerized it was evident that the will to meaning is more than just the wishful thinking of some idealists.

Research conducted by S. Kratochvil and I. Planova of the Department of Psychology of the University of Brno, Czechoslovakia, offered evidence that "the will to meaning is really a specific need not reducible to other needs, and is in greater or smaller degree present in all human beings. The relevance of the frustration of this need," the authors continue, "was documented also by case material, concerning neurotic and depressive patients. In some cases the frustration of the will to meaning had a relevant role as an etiological factor in the origin of the neurosis or of the suicidal attempt." Abraham H. Maslow goes further; to him the will to meaning is more than "an irreducible need"—he sees it as "man's primary concern."[5]

If there were still a need to demonstrate that the concept of a will to meaning has a realistic basis and is perfectly down to earth, one might consider the result of a survey published by the American Council on Education: Among the 171,509 students screened, the highest goal— held by 68.1 percent—was "developing a meaningful philosophy of life."[6] Another statistical survey, conducted at Johns Hopkins University and sponsored by the National Institute of Mental Health, found that among 7,948 students at 48 colleges, only 16 percent said their first goal was "making a lot of money." Seventy-eight percent of the students, however, checked "finding a purpose and meaning to my life."[7]

Seventy-eight percent . . . which, as it happens, is exactly the percentage of Polish youngsters who regarded it as their highest purpose in life "to improve their living standard." Apparently, Maslow's hierarchy of needs is applicable to the issue at hand: First one has to improve one's living standard, and only after this has been accomplished may he approach the task of "finding a purpose and meaning in his life." However, I regard this as a mistake. It goes without saying that someone who is ill wishes, in the first place, to become healthy. So health will seem to constitute his supreme goal in life. But in actual fact, it is no more than a means to an end, because health is a precondition for attaining whatever might be considered the real meaning in a given instance. In other words, in such a case it is first mandatory to inquire what is the end that stands behind the means. And an appropriate method for such an inquiry may well be some sort of a Socratic dialogue. As we see, Maslow's motivation theory does not suffice here, for what is needed is not so much the distinction between higher and lower needs but, rather, an answer to the question of whether the individual goals are mere means or meanings.[8]

In everyday life we are fully aware of this difference. If we did not recognize it, we wouldn't laugh at a comic strip that shows Snoopy complaining of his suffering from a feeling of meaninglessness and emptiness—until Charlie Brown comes in with a bowl full of dog food, and Snoopy exclaims, "Ah! Meaning!!" What makes us laugh is precisely the confusion of means and meaning: While food is certainly a necessary condition for survival, it is not a sufficient condition to endow one's life with meaning and thus relieve the sense of meaninglessness and emptiness.

The findings of the study done at Johns Hopkins University are paralleled by those from a study carried out at the University of Michigan: 1,533 working people were asked to rank various aspects of work in order of importance, and "good pay" came in a distant fifth. Small wonder that Joseph Katz of the State University of New York, reviewing some recent opinion polls, said that "the next wave of personnel entering industry will be interested in careers with meaning, not money."[9]

As we see, the will to meaning "cannot be explained away as merely philosophical apparel for traditional dynamic concepts," to quote from a study by James C. Crumbaugh.[10] In fact, "current psychodynamic theory and the therapy based on it are too narrow in scope to explain the behavior of the younger generation and reach them," as Z. J. Lipowski says.[11] What is even more important is the danger that man—and here again, particularly the younger generation—may be corrupted by being underrated. Conversely, if I am cognizant of the higher aspirations of man, such as his will to meaning, I am also able to muster and mobilize them.

I am always reminded, in this context, of the business my flight instructor calls crabbing. If there is a crosswind, say, from the north and the airport where I wish to land lies east and I fly east, I will miss my destination because my plane will drift to the southeast; so to compensate for this drift, I have to fly my plane in a direction north of my destination, and this is called "crabbing." But isn't it the same with man? Doesn't he, too, wind up at some point that is lower than his destination unless he is seen on a level that includes his higher aspirations? What did my flight instructor say? If I fly east in a so-called crosswind condition, I will land south of east; if I head north of east, I will land east. Well, if I take man as he is, I make him worse; if I take him as he ought to be, I make him become what he can be. But this is no longer something my flight instructor told me, but, rather, a literal quotation from Goethe.

If the concept of a will to meaning is idealistic at all, I would call such idealism the real realism. If we are to bring out the human potential at its best, we must first believe in its existence and presence. Otherwise man, too, will "drift"; he will deteriorate. For there is a human potential at its worst as well! And in spite of our belief in the potential humanness of man we must not close our eyes to the fact that *humane* humans are, and probably will always remain, a minority. But it is precisely for this reason that each of us is challenged to *join* the minority. Things are bad. But unless we do our best to improve them, everything will become worse.

On the one hand, the will to meaning is not only a true manifestation of man's humanness, but also—as has been substantiated by Theodore A. Kotchen—a reliable criterion of mental health. This hypothesis is supported by James C. Crumbaugh, Sister Mary Raphael, and Raymond R. Shrader, who measured the will to meaning and obtained the highest scores among well-motivated and successful professional and business populations.

On the other hand, lack of meaning and purpose is indicative of emotional maladjustment. Since Freud and Adler had to deal with neurotic patients—that is to say, with people frustrated in their will to meaning—it is understandable that they thought that man is motivated by the pleasure principle and the striving for superiority, respectively. Actually, the will to power and what one might call a will to pleasure are substitutes for a frustrated will to meaning. Evidence of the surrogate nature of the will to pleasure has been offered by statistical research. People visiting Vienna's Prater—an amusement park somewhat comparable to New York's Coney Island—proved to be more frustrated in their will to meaning than the average population of Vienna.[12]

Primarily and normally man does not seek pleasure; instead, pleasure—or, for that matter, happiness—is the side effect of living out the self-transcendence of existence. Once one has served a cause[13] or is involved in loving another human being, happiness occurs by itself. The will to pleasure, however, contradicts the self-transcendent quality of human reality. And it also defeats itself. For pleasure and happiness are by-products. Happiness must ensue. It cannot be pursued. It is the very pursuit of happiness that thwarts happiness. The more one makes happiness an aim, the more he misses the aim. And this is most conspicuous in cases of sexual neurosis such as frigidity or impotence. Sexual performance or experience is strangled to the extent to which it is made either an object of attention or an objective of intention. I have called the first "hyperreflection" and the second "hyperintention."

Hyperintention is observable even on a mass level. Just consider the emphasis that public opinion places on sexual achievement. As I have pointed out elsewhere,[14] this emphasis spawns preoccupations and apprehensions. People are overly concerned with sexual success and ridden with the fear of sexual failure. But fear tends to bring about precisely that of which one is afraid. Thus a vicious circle is established. And it accounts for much of the caseload regarding sexual neuroses that confronts psychiatrists today.

What is behind the emphasis on sexual achievement and power, what is behind this will to sexual pleasure and happiness, is again the frustrated will to meaning. Sexual libido only hypertrophies in an existential vacuum. The result is an inflation of sex; and like inflation on the money market, it is associated with a devaluation. More specifically, sex is devalued because it is dehumanized. Human sex is always more than mere sex.[15] And it is more than mere sex precisely to the extent that it serves as *the physical expression* of *something metasexual*—the physical expression of love. And only to the extent that sex carries out this function of embodying—incarnating—love, only to this extent will it climax in a truly rewarding experience. Seen in this light, Maslow was justified when he pointed out that those people who cannot love never get the same thrill out of sex as those who can love.

Therefore we would have to recommend that sex be rehumanized if only for the purpose of maximizing one's orgasm. This was recently substantiated by a report on 20,000 responses to 101 questions about sexual attitudes and practices; it revealed that among the factors contributing to high orgasm and potency rates, the most important one was "romanticism."[16]

And yet it is not quite accurate to say that human sex is more than mere sex. As the ethologist Irenaeus Eibl-Eibesfeldt has shown, in some vertebrates sexual behavior serves group cohesion, and this is particularly the case in man's biological ancestors—those primates that live in groups. Thus in certain apes sexual intercourse sometimes serves a social purpose exclusively. In humans, Eibl-Eibesfeldt states, there is no doubt that sexual intercourse serves not only the propagation of the species, but also the monogamous relation between the partners.

It goes without saying that the sexual instinct cannot in itself be distinctly human. After all, it is not only a property of human beings but is shared by animals as well. So let us more cautiously say that in man the sexual instinct is humanized to a higher or a lower degree, as the case may be; in him the sexual instinct approaches and approximates the potential of human sex only successively—and, as we have seen, the potential of human sex consists in its becoming an embodiment of love.

This sexual maturation is characterized by three developmental stages. The first two can be understood along the lines of Freud's differentiation between the goal of an instinct and the instinct's object. At the immature level, only a goal is sought, and the goal is tension reduction irrespective of the way in which it is accomplished. Masturbation may do. According to Freud the mature stage is reached as soon as the sexual instinct centers on normal sexual intercourse, which presupposes an object. As I see it, however, the object is not enough to guarantee a mature sexual life. For as long as an individual uses a partner simply for the purpose of reducing tension, he really "masturbates on the partner," as our patients so often say. To the individual who really is mature, the partner is in no way a means to an end. The mature individual's partnership moves on a human level, and the human level precludes the mere use of others. On the human level, I do not use another human being but I encounter him, which means that I fully recognize his humanness; and if I take another step by fully recognizing, beyond his humanness as a human being, his uniqueness as a person, it is even more than an encounter—what then takes place is love.[17]

Grasping the uniqueness of a partner understandably results in a monogamous partnership. There are no longer interchangeable partners. Conversely, if one is not able to love, he winds up with promiscuity. As masturbation means being content with tension reduction as a goal, so promiscuity means being contented with the partner as an object. In neither case is the human potential of sex actualized.

As long as one remains at the mere goal level, one's sexual instinct may be catered to by pornography; and as long as he stays at the mere object level his sexual instinct may be catered to by prostitutes. Thus, promiscuity and pornography are the marks of fixation at, or regression to, immature levels of development. Therefore it is not wise publicly to glorify the indulgence in such patterns of regressive behavior by confusing it with a progressive mentality. As to pornography, I detest the invocation of "freedom from censorship" when what is really meant is simply the freedom to make money. As compared with the hypocrisy of businessmen working in the field of so-called sex education, I praise the honesty of the call girls who bluntly confess that they are only out to make money through sex. And as to promiscuity, it not only is a type of regressive behavior but also contradicts the humanness of man. But sexual promiscuity is promulgated together with sexual intimacy, and the latter is even believed to be the answer to the ills of our age. However, I think that what is needed in this age of population explosion is existential privacy rather than sexual intimacy.[18]

Speaking of population explosion, I would like to touch on the Pill. It is not only counteracting the population explosion but, as I see it, rendering an even greater service. If it is true that it is love that makes sex human, the Pill allows for a truly human sexual life, one in which, freed from its automatic connection with procreation, sex can realize its highest potential as one of the most direct and meaningful expressions of love. Sex is human if it is experienced as a vehicle of love, and to make it into a mere means to an end contradicts the humanness of sex, regardless of whether the pleasure principle dictates the end or the procreation instinct does so. As to the latter, sex has been emancipated, thanks to the Pill, and has thereby become capable of achieving its potential status as a human phenomenon.

Today the will to meaning is often frustrated. In logotherapy one speaks of existential frustration. We psychiatrists are confronted more than ever before with patients who are complaining of a *feeling of futility* that at present plays at least as important a role as did the *feeling of inferiority* in Alfred Adler's time. Let me just quote from a letter I recently received from a young American student: "I am a 22-year-old with degree, car, security and the availability of more sex and power than I need. Now I have only to explain to myself what it all means." However, such people are complaining not only of a sense of meaninglessness but also of emptiness, and that is why I have described this condition in terms of the "existential vacuum."

There is no doubt that the existential vacuum is increasing and spreading. According to a report I was shown recently, the percentage of those suffering from it, among a population of 500 Viennese youngsters, has increased within the last two years from 30 percent to 80 percent. Even in Africa the existential vacuum is spreading, particularly among the academic youth.[19] Also, Freudians are fully aware of this phenomenon, and so are Marxists. At an international meeting of psychoanalysts it was stated that ever more patients are suffering from a lack of life content, rather than clinical symptomatology, and that this state of affairs may well account for so-called interminable analyses because, as the Freudians have contended, in such cases the psychoanalytic treatment becomes the only life content available to the patient. As to the Marxists, only recently the head of the department of psychotherapy at Karl Marx University in Leipzig confessed to the frequency of the existential vacuum as substantiated by her own investigations. As the head of the psychiatry department at a Czech university puts it, the existential vacuum is passing the borders between capitalist and Communist countries "without a visa."[20]

If asked for a brief explanation, I would say that the existential vacuum derives from the following conditions. Unlike an animal, man is not told by drives and instincts what he must do. And in contrast to man in former times, he is no longer told by traditions and values what he should do. Now, knowing neither what he must do nor what he should do, he sometimes does not even know what he basically wishes to do. Instead, he wishes to do what other people do—which is conformism—or he does what other people wish him to do—which is totalitarianism.

In addition to these two effects of the existential vacuum, there is a third, namely, neuroticism. The existential vacuum per se is not a neurosis, at least not in the strictly clinical sense. If it is a neurosis at all it would have to be diagnosed as a *sociogenic neurosis*. However, there are also cases in which the existential vacuum results in clinical symptomatology. Such patients are suffering from what I have called "noögenic neurosis." James C. Crumbaugh must be credited with having developed a special diagnostic test to differentiate the noögenic from other forms of neurosis. Scores of research projects have been based on his PIL Test. The results thereby obtained indicate that about 20 percent of the neuroses one encounters are noögenic in nature and origin. Elisabeth S. Lukas, although using a different test (her Logo-Test), has arrived at the same percentage as Crumbaugh.

As to the existential vacuum, however, which in itself is not a neurosis, a statistical survey recently showed that among my European students, 25 percent had themselves had this "abyss experience," as it may be called in contradistinction to the "peak experience." Among my American students it was not 25 but 60 percent.

A Communist psychiatrist found that among various populations of Czech students the percentage of those who had experienced the existential vacuum as measured by Crumbaugh's test was even higher than that observed and reported among students in the United States. A year later, however, the figure had become markedly lower. During that intervening year, most of the students had become involved in Dubček's movement, his battle for political liberalization and for the humanization of communism. They had been given a cause for which to fight, for which to live, and unfortunately, for which to die.

On the average, however, the fact remains that in America the existential vacuum is more manifest than in Europe. As I see it, this is due to the exposure of the average American student to an indoctrination along the lines of reductionism. To cite an instance, there is a book in which man is defined as "nothing but a complex biochemical mechanism powered by a combustion system which energizes computers with prodigious storage facilities for retaining encoded information." Or to quote another example, man is defined as a "naked ape." By offering our students such reductionist concepts of man we are reinforcing their existential vacuum. I well remember how I felt when I was a 13-year-old junior-high-school student and our natural science teacher told us that life in the final analysis was "nothing but a combustion process, an oxidation process." I sprang to my feet and said, "Professor, if this is the case, what meaning then does life have?" To be sure, in his case reductionism had taken on the form of "oxidationism," one might say.

A study of physicians by R. N. Gray and associates showed that during medical school cynicism as a rule increases, while humanitarianism decreases.[21] Only after completion of medical studies is this trend reversed, but unfortunately not in all subjects. Small wonder, I would say. Just consider the two definitions offered by the author in whose paper this study was quoted. Man is defined as nothing but "an adaptive control system," and values are defined as nothing but "homeostatic restraints in a stimulus-response process."[22] According to another reductionist definition, values are nothing but reaction formations and defense mechanisms. As for myself, I am not prepared to live for the sake of my reaction formations, even less to die for the sake of my defense mechanisms.

Here is another illustration regarding reductionism. A famous Freudian psychoanalyst devoted two volumes to Goethe. "In the 1,538 pages," a review of the book reads, "the author portrays to us a genius with the ear-marks of a manic-depressive, paranoid, and epileptoid disorder, of homosexuality, incest, voyeurism, exhibitionism, fetishism, impotence, narcissism, obsessive-compulsive neurosis, hysteria, megalomania, etc. He seems to focus almost exclusively upon the instinctual dynamic forces that underlie the artistic product. We are led to believe that Goethe's work is but the result of pre-genital fixations. His struggle does not really aim for an ideal, for beauty, for values, but for the overcoming of an embarrassing problem of premature ejaculation."[23] How wise and cautious was Freud, as compared with his epigones, when he remarked that sometimes a cigar may be a cigar and nothing but a cigar. To be sure, a Freudian would have to interpret Freud's statement as a rationalization of his cigar smoking.

The reductionist interpretation of values is likely to undermine and erode the enthusiasm of youth. As an example, let me report the following observation. A young American couple who had served as Peace Corps volunteers in Africa returned completely fed up and disgusted. At the outset they had had to participate in mandatory group sessions led by a psychologist who played a game somewhat as follows:

"Why did you join the Peace Corps?"

"We wanted to help people less privileged."

"So you must be superior to them."

"In a way."

"So there must be in you, in your unconscious, a need to prove to yourself that you are superior."

"Well, we never thought of it that way, but you are a psychologist, you certainly know better."

And so it went on. They were indoctrinated in the interpretation of their idealism and altruism as mere personal hang-ups. Even worse, they "were constantly on each other's backs, playing the 'what's *your* hidden motive' game," according to their report.

For a long time psychoanalysis has understood itself in terms of depth psychology, and depth psychology in turn has seen its assignment as the "unmasking" of unconscious dynamics underlying human behavior. Perhaps this is best illustrated by what Joseph Wilder once

called the shortest psychiatric joke he had ever
encountered:

"Are you a psychiatrist?"

"Why do you ask?"

"You're a psychiatrist."

By attempting to unmask the man who had asked
him a question, the psychiatrist really unmasked himself.
Now, unmasking is perfectly legitimate, but I would say
that it must stop as soon as one confronts what is genuine,
genuinely human, in man. If it does not stop there, the only
thing that the "unmasking psychologist" really unmasks is
his own "hidden motive"—namely, his unconscious need
to debase and depreciate the humanness of man.

At that point hyperinterpretation, as I would call it,
begins, and it proves to be most dangerous when it comes
to self-interpretation. We psychiatrists have met many
patients who are suffering from, and crippled by, the
obsessive compulsion to analyze themselves, to observe
and watch themselves, to reflect upon themselves. The
cultural climate that prevails in the United States provides
dangerous opportunity for this compulsion to become a
collective obsessive neurosis. Just consider a recent study by
Edith Weisskopf-Joelson and associates.[24] It shows that the
value that ranks highest among American college students
is self-interpretation.[25] I see in these findings another
indication of the existential vacuum. As the boomerang
returns to the hunter only when it has missed its target, so
man returns to himself, reflects upon himself, and becomes
overly concerned with self-interpretation only when he has,
as it were, missed his target, having been frustrated in his
search for meaning. What comes to mind is the Freudians'
experience with patients in whom, owing to the lack of life
content, the psychoanalytic treatment has become a substitute for that content.

Now let us turn from the causes to the effects of the
existential vacuum, inasmuch as these go beyond both

the noögenic neurosis and the feeling of meaninglessness that is to be diagnosed as a sociogenic neurosis. Among the worldwide effects is what one might call the *mass neurotic triad*, which consists of *depression, addiction,* and *aggression.* I once took a taxi to a university whose student body had invited me to give a lecture on the question of whether "the new generation is mad." I asked the cab driver to answer that question. He came up with the following succinct statement: "Of course they are mad; they kill themselves, they kill each other, and they take dope."

As to the first aspect of this triad, depression often results in suicide, and there is ample evidence that, particularly among the young generation, the number of suicides is increasing. "Suicide, which once ranked twenty-second on the list of causes of death in the United States, now rates tenth, and in some states, sixth. And for everyone who succeeds in committing suicide, fifteen will have tried and failed." What is even more important, "suicide rates among young people have risen dramatically. While suicide is listed as the tenth leading cause of death in the United States, it is third now among youth fifteen to nineteen years old, and second among college students."[26]

The spreading existential frustration lies at the root of this phenomenon. In fact, a study conducted at Idaho State University revealed that 51 of 60 students (85 percent) who had seriously attempted suicide reported as the reason that "life meant nothing" to them. Of these 51 students, 48 (94 percent) were in excellent physical health, were actively engaged socially, were performing well academically, and were on good terms with their family groups.[27]

In this context I would like to quote from a letter an American medical student recently wrote to me: "All around me here in the U.S. I see young people my age who are desperately groping for a meaning to their existence. One of my best friends died as a result of his search. I know

now that if he were here now I could help him, thanks to your book, but he is not. His death, however, will always serve to pull me toward all people who are in distress. I think this is the most powerful motivation anyone can have. I have found a meaning (despite my deep sorrow and guilt) in my friend's life and death. If I can be strong enough in the future as a medical doctor to do my job and fulfill my responsibility, his death will not have been in vain. I want more than anything to prevent this tragedy from happening to others."

Small wonder that people who are caught in the existential vacuum are eager, if meanings cannot be acquired, to provide themselves at least with mere *feelings* of meaningfulness—such as those that are available in that state of intoxication that is induced by LSD. In such states suddenly the world takes on infinite meaningfulness. But the shortcut finally proves to be a dead end, for it might well be that people who resort to LSD wind up in the long run like the experimental animals used in self-stimulation experiments. Researchers inserted electrodes into the hypothalamuses of rats, and whenever they closed the electric circuit, the rats to all appearances experienced either sexual orgasm or the satisfaction of eating. When the rats then learned to jump on the lever and by so doing to close the electric circuit themselves, they became addicted to the business and pressed the lever up to 50,000 times a day. What I regard as most remarkable is that these animals then neglected the real sexual partners and the real food that were offered to them. And I think that the "acidheads" who confine themselves to the mere feelings of meaningfulness may bypass the true meanings that are in store for them, to be fulfilled by them out in the world rather than within their own psyches.

Since I advanced this hypothesis regarding the real source from which the drug scene derives, numerous authors have written about the feeling of meaninglessness of life as it is reported by young people involved with drugs. Dr. Betty Lou Padelford points out that "The lack of a strong father figure with whom the young male could identify was felt by many authorities to be a precondition to illicit drug involvement." However, the data generated by her own study *"failed* to identify significant differences between the extent of drug involvement reported by students having a weak father image as opposed to students having a strong father image."[28] The subjects studied in her investigation were 416 students, and a significant inverse relationship between drug involvement and purpose in life was found beyond reasonable doubt ($r = -.23; p <.001$). The mean drug-involvement index for students with low purpose in life (8.90) was found to differ significantly from the mean drug-involvement index for students with high purpose in life (4.25).

Dr. Padelford also reviews the literature in the field that, along with her own research, confirms the existential vacuum hypothesis. She reports that Nowlis addressed the question of why students were interested in and took drugs. Among the reasons often listed was "the desire to find meaning in life." One of the epidemiological studies conducted for the National Commission on Marijuana and Drug Abuse was a survey of 455 students in the San Diego area, made by Judd *et al.* Users of both marijuana and hallucinogens indicated that they were bothered by and had suffered over the lack of meaning of life more than had nonusers. Another study reported in the literature was conducted by Mirin *et al.*, who found that heavy use was correlated with the search for meaningful experience and diminished goal-directed activity. Linn surveyed 700 undergraduates at the University of Wisconsin, Milwaukee, in 1968 and reported that marijuana users, compared with nonusers, were more concerned about the meaning of life. Krippner *et al.* theorized that drug use may be a form of self-administered psychotherapy for people with existential problems, e.g., the 100 percent positive response to "have things seemed meaningless to you?"[29] Shean and Fechtman found that students who had smoked marijuana regularly over a six-month period scored significantly lower (p <.001) on Crumbaugh's PIL Test than did the nonusers.[30]

In another area, i.e., the addiction to alcohol, parallel findings were published by, among others, Annemarie Von Forstmeyer, who has shown that 18 out of 20 alcoholics looked upon their existence as meaningless and without purpose.[31] Accordingly, logotherapeutically oriented techniques proved superior to other forms of therapy. James C. Crumbaugh measured existential vacuum to compare the outcome of group logotherapy with results achieved by an alcoholic treatment unit and a marathon therapy program. "Only logotherapy showed a statistically significant improvement."[32] That logotherapy equally lends itself to the treatment of drug addiction has been shown by Alvin R. Fraiser at the Narcotic Addict Rehabilitation Center at Norco, California. From 1966 to the present, he has used logotherapy in working with narcotic addicts. "As a result of this approach," he says, "I have become the only counselor in the history of the institution to have three consecutive years of the highest success rate (success meaning that the addict is not returned to the institution within one year after release). My approach to dealing with the addict has resulted in a three-year 40 percent success rate as compared to an institutional average of about 11 percent (using the established approach)."

As to the last aspect of the triad, aggression, for too long a time research in human behavior has been based on a mechanistic concept of aggression. This approach still adheres to an old-fashioned, out-dated motivation theory that depicts man as a being to whom the world ultimately serves as a mere tool for the reduction of the tensions aroused and created by libidinal or aggressive impulses. However, in contrast to this closed-system concept, man is actually a being who is reaching out for meanings to fulfill and other human beings to encounter. And certainly these fellow beings, his partners, mean more to him than just a means to the end of living out his aggressive and sexual drives and instincts. However, regarding the alternative to living them out—that is, the possibility of sublimating them—Carolyn Wood Sherif has warned us of the dangers of harboring an illusion that is so characteristic of all the closed-system concepts of man, namely, the illusion that aggression can be drained by being turned to harmless activities, such as sports. On the contrary, "there is a substantial body of research evidence that the successful execution of aggressive actions, far from reducing subsequent aggression, is the best way to increase the frequency of aggressive responses (such studies have included both animal and human behavior)."[33]

Fredrick Wertham, in his "Critique of the Report to the Surgeon General from The Committee on Television and Social Behavior," ridicules "the old getting-rid-of-aggression notion" according to which "we 'need' TV violence to relieve violent impulses and thus 'spare us real violence.' Clinical studies have revealed the adverse effects on children and youth of television violence, brutality, and sadism. TV violence was found in hundreds of cases to have harmful effects."[34] The President's Commission on the Causes and Prevention of Violence stated that the "constant diet of violent behavior on television has an adverse effect on human character and attitudes." "Reduction of violence in entertainment media would," therefore, "be of benefit," says Jerome D. Frank.[35] The *British Journal of Psychiatry* describes an experiment during the course of which "children were shown films portraying aggressive acts," and it was found that "increases in aggression occurred consistently over and above the initial tendency to behave in that way."[36] John P. Murray of the National Institute of Mental Health summarizes the results of a number of studies as follows: "viewing televised violence causes the viewer to become more aggressive."[37]

Again, upon closer investigation, one may find that not only sexual libido thrives in an existential vacuum, but also aggressive "destrudo." Statistical evidence is favorable to my hypothesis that people are most likely to become aggressive when they are caught in this feeling of emptiness and meaninglessness. Robert Jay Lifton seems to agree with me when stating that "men are most apt to kill when they feel overcome by meaninglessness."[38] According to the research conducted by W. A. M. Black and R. A. M. Gregson, recidivists differ significantly from first-sentence prisoners, who in turn differ from normals with respect to purpose in life $(p < 0.0005)$. The authors conclude that "criminality and purpose in life are inversely related. The irony is that the more persistently a man offends, the more likely he is to be sentenced to increasing terms of imprisonment and the less likely he is to increase his sense of purpose in life, and so the more likely he is to continue offending when released."[39]

In the light of such facts it is understandable that Louis S. Barber holds that logotherapy is "particularly applicable to the treatment of juvenile delinquents." For several years he has worked with young people in a rehabilitation setting. Almost always the "lack of meaning and purpose in their lives" appeared to be present. "We have one of the highest rehabilitation rates in the U.S.," Barber says, "a recidivism rate of less than 17 percent (against an average of some 40 percent)." This program "builds responsibility within each of the boys. It is logo-education in practice." That "a logotherapeutic approach offers great possibilities to the field of rehabilitation" is evidenced by a mean increase in the will to meaning from 86.13 to 103.46 (within four months, at that) among the juvenile delinquents who were subject to Dr. Barber's treatment.

How, then, can psychotherapy at large cope with the mass neurotic triad: How can it tackle depression, addiction, and aggression as they afflict mankind? If we include in the pathology of humanity what really is not neurosis in the strictly clinical sense but, rather, a para-clinical phenomenon, we are justified in speaking of a neuroticization of humanity. Now, it is my contention that the *deneuroticization of humanity* requires a *rehumanization of psychotherapy*.

If one is to overcome the ailments of this age, one must properly understand them—that is to say, understand them as the effects of frustration. And if one is to understand the frustrations of man, one has to understand his motivations, to begin with, and especially the most human of human motivations, which is man's search for meaning. This, however, is not possible unless psychotherapy detaches itself from its own reductionism. Everything short of a rehumanized psychotherapy would reinforce the mass neurotic triad. Consider the three aspects of reductionism—subjectivism, homeostasis, and pan-determinism—and let us ask ourselves: If meanings and values really are "nothing but" defense mechanisms and reaction formations, as the psychodynamically oriented theories have it, is life really worth living? Isn't it rather understandable if I am submerged in depression and wind up with suicide? As to addiction: If man really is just seeking pleasure and happiness by gratifying his needs in order to get rid of the tensions created by them, why worry? Why not build up perpetual and perfect tranquility by simply taking drugs? And finally, regarding aggression: If I really am the victim of outer and inner circumstances and influences—the product of environment and heredity—and my behavior, decision, and action are "nothing but" the result of operant conditioning, conditioned reflexes, and learning processes, who is justified to demand that I improve or to expect that I change? There is no need for apologies; there are plenty of excuses; there are alibis. And as for myself, I am neither free nor responsible. So there is no reason why I should not continue living out the aggressive impulses about which I can do nothing anyway.

From all this it should be clear that we are in dire need of a rehumanization of psychotherapy unless we wish to reinforce, rather than counteract, the ills of our age. So let us briefly review the path that psychotherapy has taken since the time of Freud, with a view to an exploration of the factors that are likely to account for a dehumanization of psychotherapy.

Freud's psychoanalysis teaches how to *unmask the neurotic*, how to determine the hidden, unconscious dynamics underlying his behavior. This behavior is analyzed, and "analyzing" in this context means interpreting. Later on, however, the assumption of the unconscious was "used as a carte blanche on which almost any casual explanation could be written," to quote from an article published in *Psychology Today*. Explanatory devices, some skeptical therapists argued, "as often as not actually cover up rather than reveal the empirical data."

In contradistinction, and counteraction, to the psychoanalytic system, Carl Rogers's approach to counseling is characterized by restraint from being directive and abstention from interpretations. After all, interpretation along the lines of the psychoanalytic system is based on free associations. However, they are "never truly 'free,'" to quote Judd Marmor. Rather, they are influenced by the analysts, and the patients are indoctrinated in a very specific *Weltanschauung* or ideology. According to the particularly Freudian psychoanalytic ideology, man is ultimately nothing but a being ruled and governed by the homeostasis principle; human love is nothing but the expression of a sublimated and aim-inhibited sexual drive; and as for personal conscience, that is no more than one's superego or the introjection of his father image. It is in this area that Rogers's principal merit lies, for I would say that it is to his credit to have shown us how to *de-ideologize psychotherapy*.

Moreover, "in the past ten years the prestige of psychoanalysis has dropped significantly in academic and scientific circles," according to Marmor, because "over the years psychoanalysis has been oversold as an optimal psychotherapeutic technique. Whether or not classical psychoanalysis is truly the optimal approach for any specific form of psychopathology still remains to be conclusively proved," Marmor believes, since "at best it is indicated in only a small proportion of cases."[40]

Of course, the question may be asked why psychoanalysis still "is in a position to perpetuate its theories, proven or unproven," and T. P. Millar offers the following explanation:

> The voice of dissent is not easily heard in psychiatric America. We are in an era when the *sine qua non* of publication in many a psychiatric journal is a dynamic formulation of the problem in oral, anal or Oedipal terms. We are in an era when to disagree with psychoanalysis is more liable to lead to a gratuitous diagnosis and dynamic formulation of the disagreer than it is to an examination of the arguments advanced. Indeed, by diagnosing the opposition, the ideas advanced are rendered grist for the interpretative mill rather than propositions to be refuted. But can it be that only psychoanalysts have *opinions* while the rest of us have *problems*? Dr. Burness Moore, chairman of the American Psychoanalytic Association's public information committee, writes in that Association's newsletter: "Indeed, there is indication of

increasing derogation of analysis in the past few years," and the Association has hired a public relations consultant.

"This," Millar comments, "may indeed be the appropriate action, but it does seem possible that more might be accomplished if psychoanalysis were to undertake to rehabilitate its theory rather than its public image."[41]

However, psychoanalysis had already lost much of its territory to a sound and sober trend in the field of psychotherapy, namely, behavior therapy. As early as 1960, H. J. Eysenck deplored "the lack of experimental or clinical evidence in favor of psychoanalysis." The theories of psychoanalysis are "beliefs" with which "psychiatrists in training are now frequently indoctrinated." However, Eysenck argues not only in general that "Freudian theories are outside the realm of science" but also in particular that "so-called symptomatic cures can be achieved which are long-lasting and do not produce alternative symptoms." This fact "argues strongly against the Freudian hypothesis." In contrast to the Freudian "belief," Eysenck thinks that abolition of the symptoms does not at all "leave behind some mysterious complex seeking outlet in alternative symptoms."[42]

Long before this, logotherapy also had offered evidence that neuroses need not in each and every case be traced to the Oedipal situation or other types of conflicts and complexes but may derive from feedback mechanisms such as the circle formation built up by anticipatory anxiety.[43] And as early as 1947 I myself attempted to interpret neurosis in reflexological terms when pointing out that

> all psychoanalytically oriented psychotherapies are mainly concerned with uncovering the primary conditions of the "conditioned reflex," which neurosis can be understood to be, and "the primary conditions" are represented by the situation—outer and inner—in which a given neurotic symptom

emerged for the first time. It is my contention, however, that the full-fledged neurosis is not only caused by the *primary conditions* but also by *secondary conditioning*. This *reinforcement*, in turn, is caused by the feedback mechanism called anticipatory anxiety. Therefore, if we wish to *recondition* a conditioned reflex, we must break the vicious cycle formed by anticipatory anxiety, and this is the very job done by the logotherapeutic "paradoxical intention" technique.[44]

It is my contention that behavior therapy has made a valuable contribution to the evolution of psychotherapy in that it has shown how to *demythologize neurosis*. This formulation is not too far-fetched when one considers the fact that Sigmund Freud himself described his instinct theory as a "mythology" and the instincts as "mythical" entities.

To sum up, Freud has unmasked the neurotic; Rogers has de-ideologized psychotherapy; and Eysenck, Wolpe, and others have demythologized neurosis; and yet a discontent remains. Even to such a declared materialist as Christa Kohler, who runs the department of psychotherapy at Karl Marx University in Leipzig, "the behavioristically oriented psychotherapists Wolpe and Eysenck" are, to her mind, excessively "sliding into a biologistic and mechanistic position."[45] She may be right. Particularly in an era such as ours, one of meaninglessness, depersonalization, and dehumanization, it is not possible to cope with the ills of the age unless the human dimension, the dimension of human phenomena, is included in the concept of man, which indispensably underlies every sort of psychotherapy, be it on the conscious or unconscious level.

Nikolaus Petrilowitsch of the department of psychiatry at the University of Mainz, Germany, has drawn attention to the fact that logotherapy—in contrast to all other schools of psychotherapy—does not remain in the dimension of neurosis. What does he mean? Psychoanalysis sees in neurosis the result of certain psychodynamics that it counteracts by bringing into play, say, transference, which, to be sure, is another sort of psychodynamics. And as to behavior therapy, it sees neurosis as the result of conditioning, of certain learning processes, and counteracts these by means of reconditioning processes, relearning. But logotherapy, as Petrilowitsch sees it, goes beyond the plane of neurosis and opens up the dimension of human phenomena, thereby placing itself in a position to tap and draw upon the resources that are available in this dimension—resources such as the uniquely human capacities of self-transcendence and what I have come to call "self-detachment."

Petrilowitsch now credits logotherapy for having *rehumanized psychotherapy* so that, after the unmasking of the neurotic, the de-ideologizing of psychotherapy, and the demythologizing of neurosis, the rehumanizing of psychotherapy has been arrived at, or at least is under way.[46]

But now let us come back for a moment to the two uniquely human capacities of self-transcendence and self-detachment. The latter signifies the capacity to detach oneself from oneself. Paradoxical intention—a logotherapeutic technique that lends itself to the short-term treatment of obsessive-compulsive and phobic neuroses—is intended to muster and mobilize self-detachment in general. In particular, however, it utilizes a unique and specific aspect of self-detachment, namely, the human sense of humor. Small wonder that, by methodologically including this important facet of man's humanness in its armamentarium, logotherapy acquires an additional asset over behavior therapy. This does not detract from the fact that techniques that parallel paradoxical intention are applied and used in behavior modification. But it is remarkable and noteworthy that Dr. Iver Hand of London's Maudsley Hospital found that patients who had been treated along the lines of behavior therapy in a group setting "used humor spontaneously as one of their main coping mechanisms."[47] Other behavioristically oriented authors such as L. Solyom, J. Garza-Perez, B. L. Ledwidge, and C. Solyom not only successfully applied paradoxical intention but also offered statistical and even experimental evidence that it really works and that the therapeutic results obtained by this logotherapeutic technique cannot be dismissed as the effects of mere suggestion.[48]

By and large, obsessive-compulsive and phobic neuroses are psychogenic as opposed to noögenic, so one may say that invoking the human potential of self-detachment is instrumental in the therapy of psychogenic neuroses. Cognizance of self-transcendence, however, is indispensable in the diagnosis of noögenic neuroses. The noögenic neurosis is the effect of a frustration of the will to meaning, which in turn is a manifestation of self-transcendence.

Self-transcendence and self-detachment are irreducibly human phenomena and are exclusively available in the human dimension. From this it follows that we cannot really help man in his predicament if we insist that our concept of man be patterned after the "machine model" or after the "rat model," as Gordon W. Allport mockingly put it. After all, there are no computers that laugh at themselves, nor are there animals that care about meaning and purpose in their existence.

The engineering approach to the patient as a machine to repair or a mechanism to fix may by itself be detrimental. It may debilitate the patient's awareness of himself as a free and responsible agent. In other words, it may eventuate in an iatrogenic neurosis—a neurosis that is caused by the physician. Because in this case the doctor is a psychiatrist, one might speak of a *psychiatrogenic neurosis*. The psychotherapist must therefore reexamine the philosophical underpinnings of whatever approach he adopts, lest he inflict such a psychiatrogenic neurosis on the patient. This is the reason why logotherapy is not only a successful therapeutic procedure in noögenic, sociogenic, and psychogenic cases but also a prophylactic measure with respect to psychiatrogenic neuroses.

We have heard that man is a being in search of meaning. We have seen that today his search is unsatisfied and that this constitutes the pathology of our age. The time has come to ask ourselves, What is the therapeutic approach? In order to answer this question, we must focus first on another one; namely, how does this meaning-seeking being search for meaning, and also, how does he manage to find it? There is no doubt that meaning must be found and cannot be given. Least of all can it be given by us psychiatrists. We must be satisfied if our colleagues do not *take away* their patients' meaning and purpose. For example, I recently received a letter that contained the following passage: "I have had recurrent depressive states until two days ago a psychiatrist at Harvard University (where I am a student) told me bluntly . . . 'your life is meaningless, you have nothing to look forward to, I am surprised that you haven't committed suicide.'" Is this all the help a psychiatrist has to offer? I do not think so. Here is another example to which Edith Weisskopf-Joelson of the University of Georgia drew attention: "A woman suffering from an incurable cancer was comparing the fullness of her previous life with the senselessness of the ultimate phase. Thereupon a Freudian psychoanalyst countered that he believed she had made a gross mistake. 'Her life-in-general had been without meaning even before the onset of her disease. In reality, the two phases were bare of meaning and sense.'"[49]

To repeat, meaning must be found and cannot be given. To try to give meaning would amount to moralizing. I for one think that if morals are to survive they will have to be ontologized. Ontologized morals, however, will no longer define what is good and what is bad in terms of what one should do and what one must not do. What is good will be defined as that which fosters the meaning fulfillment of a being. And what is bad will be defined as that which hinders this meaning fulfillment.

To say that meaning must be found is equivalent to saying that meaning is something to discover rather than to invent. This in turn is equivalent to saying that the "demand characteristics" (Kurt Lewin) or "demand qualities" inherent in a given situation, the "requirements" of the situation, are "objective qualities."[50] Thus meanings prove to be objective, rather than merely subjective, on empirical grounds.

Consider the situation of a subject confronted with a Rorschach test. He is reading into the ink blots an entirely subjective meaning—a meaning whose very subjectiveness betrays the makeup of his personality, as is the case in any "projective" test. But life, I would say, does not compare to a Rorschach test but, rather, to what is called an "embedded figure." Here one cannot simply read a meaning into the drawing but must find out the meaning that is objectively there, even though it is hidden and therefore still to be discovered.

James C. Crumbaugh must be credited with having shown that the discovery of meaning has something to do with a gestalt perception. The will to meaning, he writes, "can be comprehended in terms of the Gestalt psychologists' laws of perceptual organization," and he "relates it to perception—the will to perceive, to read meaning into the environment, to interpret and organize stimulus elements into meaningful wholes":

> The Gestalt psychologists hold this organizational tendency to be an innate property of the mind. It has survival value, for the greater the range of stimuli which can be comprehended

and interrelated, the greater the chance of adaptive manipulation. By the will to meaning, however, Frankl implies a particular kind of perception: Man not only strives to perceive his environment as a meaningful totality, but he strives to find an interpretation which will reveal him as an individual with a purpose to fulfill in order to complete this total Gestalt—he strives to find an *apologia pro vita sua*, a justification for his existence. The Gestalt laws of organization, subsumed under the law of *Prägnanz*, or filledness, represent an unlearned striving to construct meaningful, unified Gestalten from all elements of experience. Frankl's will to meaning can be considered another way of looking at the same concept, though there is an advantage in his thinking, for it is a particularly human idea, pointing up man's distinctive ability to perceive or find meaning not merely in what is, but in what can be. This is the ability which Max Scheler has called the capacity for free contemplation of the possible, and which he considers the factor that separates man from the lower animals.

Crumbaugh concludes by pointing out that

evidence favorable to Frankl's postulated drive would be found in the accumulated evidence of the Gestalt leaders, principally Koffka and Köhler, for the Gestalt laws of organization. As previously noted, the will to meaning is primarily a perceptual phenomenon. It follows that if innate tendencies toward perceptual organization exist, it may be claimed that they manifest a striving toward organization of experience into ontologically significant patterns.[51]

So meaning must be found and cannot be given. And it must be found by oneself, by one's own conscience. Conscience may be defined as a means to discover meanings, to "sniff them out," as it were. In fact, conscience lets us arrive at the unique meaning gestalts dormant in all the unique situations that form a string called a man's life. Insofar as the perception of such meaning gestalts boils down to the interpretation of given life situations, Karl Barth was right when he said that "conscience is the true interpreter of life." And if we now ask ourselves by what man is led and guided in his search for meaning, certainly this function is carried out by conscience.

Conscience is a human phenomenon, and we must see to it that it is preserved in its humanness rather than being dealt with reductionistically. Reductionism is a pseudoscientific procedure that either reduces human phenomena to, or deduces them from, subhuman phenomena. For example, conscience is reductionistically interpreted as nothing but the result of conditioning processes. But the behavior of a dog that has wet the carpet and now slinks under the couch with his tail between his legs does not manifest conscience but something I would rather call anticipatory anxiety—more specifically, the fearful expectation of punishment—and this might well be the result of conditioning processes. It has nothing to do with conscience, because true conscience has nothing to do with the fearful expectation of punishment. As long as a man is still motived by either the fear of punishment or the hope of reward—or, for that matter, by the wish to appease the superego—conscience has not yet had its say.

Konrad Lorenz was cautious enough to speak of "moral*analoges* Verhalten bei Tieren" (behavior in animals that is *analogous* to moral behavior in man). By contrast, the reductionists do not recognize a qualitative difference between the two types of behavior. They deny that a uniquely human phenomenon exists at all. And they do so not on empirical grounds, as one might assume, but on the basis of an a priori denial. They insist that there is nothing in man that cannot be found in animals as well. Or, to vary a well-known dictum, *nihil est in homine, quod non prius fuerit in animalibus.* This brings to mind the joke about a rabbi who was consulted by two parishioners. One man contended that the other's cat had stolen and eaten up five pounds of butter. The other contended that his cat did not care for butter. "Bring me the cat," the rabbi ordered. They brought him the cat. "Now bring me scales," he continued. And they brought him scales. "How many pounds of butter did you say the cat has eaten?" he asked. "Five pounds, Rabbi," was the answer. Thereupon the rabbi put the cat on the scales and, believe it or not, it weighed exactly five pounds. "Now I have the butter," the rabbi said, "but where is the cat?" He had started with the a priori assumption that if there are five pounds, it must be five pounds of butter. But is it not the same with the reductionists? They too start with the a priori assumption that if there is anything in man, it must be possible to explain it along the lines of animal behavior. Eventually they discover in man all the conditioned reflexes, conditioning processes, innate releasing mechanisms and whatever else they have been in search of. "Now we have it," they say, like the rabbi, "but where is—man?"

Conscience is a human phenomenon, I said before, and therefore must not be dealt with reductionistically—that is to say, on a subhuman level, be it in exclusively behavioristic terms or psychodynamic ones. Nor must a neurosis stemming from the repression of conscience be treated solely on the grounds of behavioristic or psychodynamic concepts. There is a published case of "existential depression"[52] that was treated by the behavior-therapeutic technique called "thought-stopping." The patient had been suffering from "negative thoughts about himself" due to "negative self-evaluation." Since his depression was considered an "existential" one, it is fair to assume that it was his conscience that caused the negative "responses to his own behavior" and even "repeated suicide attempts." From this it follows that treating the "negative thoughts by thought-stopping procedures" amounted to a repression of conscience, which Martin Heidegger taught us to regard as a wired-in existential monitor (the over-simplification is mine).

The following is a case in which psychoanalysis rather than behavior modification induced the repression of conscience:

> Since the Summer of 1973 I have been employed as an assistant psychologist by two psychiatrists in San Diego. During my supervision sessions I often disagreed with the psychoanalytic theory that my employers sought to teach me. Yet, as their manner was very authoritarian, I was fearful of expressing my contrary opinions. I feared that I might lose my job. I therefore suppressed my own opinions to a large degree. After several months of this self-suppression, I began to feel anxiety during my supervision sessions. I began to accept the therapeutic aid of some of my friends. However, we succeeded only in making the anxiety problem worse; for what did we do but approach the problem in a somewhat psychoanalytic manner? We sought to uncover the early traumas in me that were causing my transference anxiety with my supervisors. We studied my early relationship to my father, etc., to no avail. Thus, I increasingly found myself in a state of hyperreflection, and my condition grew worse. My anxiety rose to such a level at my supervision sessions that I had to mention it to the psychiatrists in order to explain my behavior. They recommended that I see a psychoanalytically oriented psychotherapist for personal therapy in order to get to the hidden meaning of this anxiety. Not being able to afford such professional help, my friends and I increased our efforts to uncover the deep hidden meaning of my anxiety, and I became worse. I often had extreme anxiety attacks. My recovery began with Dr. Frankl's class, Man's Search for Meaning, on January 8, 1974. I heard Dr. Frankl speak of the difficulties encountered when one tries to psychoanalytically unmask an authentic response. During that four-hour class I began to see how the therapy I had undergone had increased my problem: an iatrogenic neurosis almost. I began to see that it was my own self-suppression in the supervision sessions that had caused my anxiety. My disagreement with the psychiatrists and my fear of expressing this disagreement had caused my reaction. I quickly ended the therapy and felt better

upon doing so. Yet the real change came during my next supervision session. During this session I began to express my opinions and disagreements with the psychiatrists when I actually felt such disagreements. I felt no fear of losing my job, for my peace of mind had become far more important than my job. As I began to express myself in this session, I immediately felt my anxiety beginning to decrease. In the past two weeks, my anxiety has decreased by about 90 percent.

So conscience is a human phenomenon. However, it can be an all too human phenomenon. It not only leads us to meaning but may also lead us astray. This is part and parcel of the human condition. Conscience may err, and I cannot know for certain whether my conscience is right and another's conscience, which tells him something different, is wrong, or whether the reverse is true. Not that there is no truth: there is. And there can be only one truth. But no one can be absolutely sure it is he who has arrived at this truth.

So man can only stick to his conscience, although, until he lies on his deathbed, he never knows whether it is the true meaning his conscience mediates to him. As Gordon W. Allport so beautifully put it, "we can be at one and the same time half-sure and whole-hearted."[53]

Meanings refer to unique situations—and the equally unique persons confronting them. In contrast to the meanings, which are unique, values are more or less universal in that they are shared by whole segments of a given population. I would even define values as meaning-universals. As such, however, they are subjected to changes, and even more, they are affected by the present decay of traditions. (This cultural climate, after all, is reflected and mirrored on the personal level by the feeling of meaninglessness, by the inner void, by what I have described and termed the existential vacuum.) Traditions and values are crumbling. But meanings are not—cannot be—transmitted by traditions because in contrast to values, which are universal, meanings are unique. And as such they are transmitted, mediated to one's consciousness, by personal conscience.

In an age such as ours, in the age of meaninglessness, education, instead of confining itself to transmitting traditions and knowledge, must see its principal assignment in refining the individual's conscience—his only capacity still to find meanings despite the wane of traditions and values. In other words, the crumbling of universal values can be counteracted only by finding the unique meanings. In an age in which the Ten Commandments are losing their unconditional validity in the eyes of many people, man must be equipped with the capacity to listen to and obey the ten thousand demands and commandments hidden in the ten thousand situations with which life is confronting him. And it is these demands that are revealed to him by an alert conscience. Only then, by virtue of an alert conscience, can he also resist the effects of the existential vacuum as intimated at the outset, namely, conformism and totalitarianism.

A doctor cannot give meanings to his patients. Nor can a professor give meanings to his students.[54] What they may give, however, is an example, the existential example of personal commitment to the search for truth. As a matter of fact, the answer to the question, What is the meaning of life? can only be given out of one's whole being—one's life is itself the answer to the question of its meaning. In other words, morals have to be not only ontologized but also existentialized.

It is a tenet of logotherapy that the humanness of man is grounded in his sense of responsibility.[55] Man is responsible for fulfilling the meaning of his life. Being human means responding to life situations, replying to the questions they ask. Being human means answering these calls—but who is calling? To whom is man responding? These questions cannot be answered by logotherapy. It is the patient who must answer them. Logotherapy can only heighten the patient's innate awareness of his responsibility, and this responsibility includes answering the question of how to interpret his life, that is to say whether along the lines of theism or atheism.

From this it follows that logotherapy does not at all "hover close to authoritarianism," and least of all does it amount to "taking over the patient's responsibility and diminishing him as a person."[56] On the contrary, logotherapy can be defined as education to responsibility.[57] However, I would say that at present responsibility must be defined as selectivity. We are living in an affluent society, and this is an affluence not only of material goods but of various sorts of stimuli as well. We are bombarded by the mass media. We are bombarded by sexual stimuli. And, last but not least, the information explosion represents a further, new affluence. Heaps of books and journals pile up on our desks. Unless we wish to drown in total (not only sexual) promiscuity, we have to choose between what is important and what is not, what is meaningful and what is not. We have to become selective and discriminating.

I concluded my address to the 1967 Conference of College Presidents, which was sponsored by the Institute of Higher Education of Teachers College, Columbia University, by saying, "I venture to predict here and now the surge of a new sense of responsibleness."[58] The rise of this responsibleness was noticeable particularly among the youth. I saw its first signs in the 1960s protest movements, although I frankly have to confess that much of this protesting was better described as anti-testing, because it was struggling not for something but, rather, against something. This is quite understandable, however, because the young people were caught in the existential vacuum. They did not know of anything worthy of being fought for, and there were so many things to be against. However,

I was sure that sooner or later they would come up with positive, constructive, and creative alternatives. After all, many tasks were in store for them, waiting to be completed. They had only to widen their horizons and to notice that there was much meaning to be fulfilled around them that would entail and engender a sense of coresponsibility. I remember that in Canada students were fasting, and citizens were invited to pay a certain amount for each hour that a student went without food. The students sent the money to Biafra. At the same time we had a lot of snow in Vienna, and there was a labor shortage because so few people cared to do the menial work of shoveling snow. Students from the University of Vienna volunteered to do the job and sent that money to Biafra, too. In these examples I see a growing concern with other people on a planetary level, an increasing sense of worldwide solidarity.

The emphasis that logotherapy places on respon- sibility not only awakens in the patient a growing awareness of his own responsibility, but also precludes moralizing on the part of the therapist. Logotherapy is neither teaching nor preaching. The logotherapist does not, as Rollo May says, "supply the patient with his goal."[59] If he ever has, he was no logotherapist. After all, it was not a logotherapist but the psychoanalyst whom F. Gordon Pleune described as "a moralist first and foremost."[60] And it was not logotherapy but psychoanalysis that was defined by E. Mansell Pattison as "a moral enterprise whose central concern is morality."[61] The logotherapist leaves it to the patient to decide what is meaningful and what is not, or, for that matter, what is good and what is bad. This abstinence from value judg- ments, however, is not a universally accepted principle. To quote, for a change, a representative of behavior therapy, L. Krasner states that "it is the therapist who is making decisions as to what is good and bad behavior."[62] Joseph

Wolpe and Arnold A. Lazarus "do not shrink from attacking on rational grounds a patient's religious beliefs if they are a source of suffering."[63]

The fact remains that a psychiatrist cannot show the patient what, in a given situation, the meaning is. But he may well show the patient that there is a meaning and, as we shall see, that life not only holds a meaning, a unique meaning, for each and every man, but also never ceases to hold such a meaning—retaining it literally up to the last moment, to one's last breath. The patient then will see a meaning in his life under any conditions. In a word, he will become, and be, aware that the meaning of life is an unconditional one.

What we here embark on is not a value judgment of facts but rather factual statements about values. What we are engaged in is the phenomenological analysis of the valuing process as it goes on in the man in the street (who has not been exposed to *reductionist indoctrination*, be it on American campuses or analytical couches) whenever he sets out to find the meaning of his life. And the unbiased man in the street, indeed, does not understand himself as a battleground for the clashing claims of ego, id, and superego. Nor does he see himself as the pawn and plaything of conditioning processes or drives and instincts. By virtue of what I call the *pre-reflective ontological self-understanding,* or what is also called "the wisdom of the heart," he knows that being human means being responsible for fulfilling the meaning potential inherent in a given life situation. What is even more important, the man in the street knows that meaning may be found not only in creating a work and doing a deed, not only in encountering someone and experiencing something, but also, if need be, in the way in which he stands up to suffering.

As we see, the unbiased analysis of the unbiased man in the street reveals how he actually experiences values.

Such an analysis is phenomenological, and as such it refrains from any preconceived patterns of interpretation and abstains from forcing phenomena into the Procrustean bed of pet concepts along the lines of a particular indoctrination, pet concepts such as "underlying psychodynamics" or "operant conditioning."

The phenomenological analysis of the man in the street yields those immediate data of experience from which, eventually, an entire axiology may be derived. Specifically, three chief groups of values may be discerned. I have classified them in terms of creative, experiential, and attitudinal values. As a matter of fact, it is only on the basis of this axiological trichotomy that life's unconditional meaningfulness can be maintained. It is through attitudinal values that even the negative, tragic aspects of human existence, or what I call the "tragic triad"—pain, guilt, and death—may be turned into something positive and creative. Caught in a hopeless situation as its helpless victim, facing a fate that cannot be changed, man still may turn his predicament into an achievement and accomplishment at the human level. He thus may bear witness to the human potential at its best, which is to turn tragedy into triumph. "The measure of a man is the way he bears up under misfortune," as Plutarch once put it.

Logotherapy is, as it were, trifocal. It focuses on three fundamental facts of human existence: a will to meaning, a meaning in suffering, and a freedom of will. As to the last, man's freedom of choice concerns the freedom to choose not only one's own way of living, but even one's own way of dying.

The logotherapeutic emphasis on the potential meaning of unavoidable suffering has nothing to do with masochism. Masochism means accepting unnecessary suffering, but I explicitly referred to "a fate that cannot be changed." What can be changed should be changed. Let

me illustrate this with an advertisement that was couched
in the following verse:

> Calmly bear, without ado,
> That which fate imposed on you;
> But to bedbugs don't resign:
> Turn for help to Rosenstein (644 W. 161 St.)!

The phenomenological analysis of the wisdom of
the heart of the man in the street discloses that he is
cognizant of creative, experiential, and attitudinal values.
Further, he knows that attitudinal values rank higher than
creative and experiential values. In other words, he also is
cognizant of their hierarchy. It is to her credit that Elisabeth
S. Lukas offered statistical evidence that the man in the
street is fully aware of both the trichotomy of values and
their hierarchy. Dr. Lukas based her research on
computerized data obtained from 1,340 subjects.

Empirical corroboration and confirmation that life is
unconditionally meaningful was contributed by some of
the several dozens of research projects that have been
based on the PIL Test developed by James C. Crumbaugh.
Thomas Yarnell's study of 40 Air Force servicemen and
40 hospitalized male schizophrenics "showed that scores
on the Purpose-in-Life Test are not related to age or
IQ."[64] "This would fit Crumbaugh's finding of no
correlation between PIL scores and educational level. It
appears then that life can be considered meaningful
regardless of age, IQ, or educational level." For the
meaning of life is unconditional ultimately with respect
to outer as well as inner conditions. S. Kratochvil and
I. Planova of the Department of Psychology, University of
Brno, Czechoslovakia, found in their research that
"unfavorable circumstances in life may but do not have to
frustrate one existentially; it depends on one's value
system"—i.e., it is dependent on whether or not one

is aware of attitudinal values as a meaning potential to fulfill, if need be.[65] As to inner conditions, Jann Ruch has shown, on the one hand, that "individuals with a wide variety of personality traits may experience meaning in life." On the other hand, "no personality trait insures against an existential vacuum."[66] In another study, authored by Joseph A. Durlak of Vanderbilt University, "a significant negative correlation was found between purpose in life and fear of death ($r = -.68$, $p < .001$). Results thus supported Frankl's notions that Ss [subjects] who reported a high purpose and meaning in their life tended to fear death less and to have a more accepting attitude toward it. In comparison, Ss who reported less purpose and meaning in their life showed a higher fear of death." It seems to be most important that the recognition of the unconditional meaningfulness of life is not even dependent on our being religious or irreligious. "It does not appear," says Durlak, "that a belief in a God and in a future existence after death could serve as an explanation for the different attitudes toward life and death found."[67]

This is perfectly in accordance with Augustine Meier's findings. His research study "indicates that the educational background and the religious affiliation of the subjects are not related to variations in the mean scores on the PIL."[68] Leonard Murphy had already "found evidence to show that people who had chosen God and [those who chose] another person as their life objective did not differ significantly in their scores on the PIL. Both groups found equal meaning for their lives."[69] In Meier's study, however, subjects were taken from five different religious denominations, and it is his contention that "the inability to find evidence to show that subjects differ on the PIL scores on the basis of religious differences gives support to Frankl's idea that God, as experienced by different religious affiliations, can give equal meaning to subjects." In addition, Meier found evidence to show that "sex and PIL are not related variables." The evidence of his study, Meier believes, "supports Frankl's idea that all people are equally capable of finding similar intensities of meaning." More specifically, evidence from Meier's study shows that "the 13–15 age group has access to experiential values in particular, the 45–55 age group appears to derive 'meaning in life' from the actualization and discovery of creative values, the 65 and over age group derives its meaning from the discovery and actualization of attitudinal values."[70]

We psychiatrists are neither teachers nor preachers but have to learn from the man in the street, from his pre-reflective ontological self-understanding, what being human is all about. We have to learn from his *sapientia cordis,* from the wisdom of his heart, that being human means being confronted continually with situations, each of which is at once a chance and a challenge, giving us a "chance" to fulfill ourselves by meeting the "challenge" to fulfill its meaning. Each situation is a call, first to listen, and then to respond.

As I see it, it is the assignment of phenomenology to translate this wisdom of the heart into scientific terms. If morals are to survive they must be not only ontologized and existentialized, but also phenomenologized. Thus the man in the street becomes the true teacher of morals.

Let me illustrate by quoting from a write-up on the seminars at the University of Chicago's Billings Hospital: "Unseen behind a one-way glass, medical students, social workers, nurses and aides, chaplains and student chaplains watch sufferers from illnesses which most often are fatal come to an understanding with death. In an entirely real sense, *the patients are teachers*—through their own experience—about the end of life."[71]

A sense of fulfillment is available to the man in the street, indeed, in the face of dying—and suffering. To demonstrate this let me again take up the letter mentioned in the preface to the first English edition (1975), received from a prisoner at the Baltimore County Prison. This was a man who was "financially ruined, in jail," and yet "at complete peace" with himself and the world after he had found a meaning in even such a miserable life. He concluded the letter by exclaiming, "how wonderful life is. I embrace today, anxiously await tomorrow."

Pre-reflective ontological self-understanding really consists of two aspects: "a prelogical understanding of being" and "a premoral understanding of meaning." In some cases, however, both aspects are repressed. Neither is compatible with indoctrination in a reductionist philosophy of life, which results in nihilism, to which the reaction is cynicism. I once had to take over the treatment of an outstanding psychoanalyst who was caught in a severe depression resulting from nihilism. It was hard to help him find his way to the existential ground on which the direction and vision of values again were available to him—available to him because he *was himself* the direction and vision. There is a point at which being and meaning merge. This, after all, is the reason why the premoral understanding of meaning is rooted in the prelogical understanding of being, and both are blended into pre-reflective ontological self-understanding.

Even in diehard positivists the wisdom of the heart may supersede the knowledge of the brain and allow for recognizing the unconditional meaningfulness of life through the potential meaning of suffering. From this I would not even exempt the nihilists. "It is strange," a graduate psychology student of the University of California at Berkeley writes in a letter to me: "The nihilists first laugh at your concept of meaning through suffering—and ultimately their tears dissolve them."

It is obvious that Nicholas Mosley was right when he wrote that "there is a subject nowadays which is taboo in the way that sexuality was once taboo, which is to talk about life as if it had any meaning."[72] It therefore is understandable that logotherapy is facing some resistance. It is no longer confronted, and concerned, with instinctual and sexual frustrations and repressions but with the frustration—and consequent repression—of the will to meaning. Not *eros* but *logos* is the victim of repression. Once the will to meaning is repressed, however, the existence of meaning is no longer perceived.

Logotherapy aims to unlock the will to meaning and to assist the patient in seeing a meaning in his life. In so doing, however, it leans on the phenomenological analysis of pre-reflective ontological self-understanding. It borrows from what the patient knows by the wisdom of his heart and in the depth of his unconscious. Through logotherapy this knowledge is brought to the surface of consciousness. And if it has been my contention that *phenomenology* means *translating* the wisdom of the heart into scientific terms, I now may add another definition: *Logotherapy* means *retranslating* this wisdom of the heart into plain words, into the language of the man in the street so that he may benefit from it. And it *is* possible to convey it to him.

Let me just restate what happened when I spoke to the prisoners of San Quentin in 1966, at the request of the prison's director. After I had addressed these prisoners, who were the toughest criminals in California, one stood up and said, "Dr. Frankl, would you be kind enough to say a few words through the mike to Aaron Mitchell, who is expecting to die in the gas chamber in a couple of days? The people on death row are not allowed to come down to the Chapel, but perhaps you will say a few words particularly to him" (an embarrassing position, but I had to accept this challenge and say a few words). I improvisingly said, "Mr. Mitchell, believe me, I understand your situation. I myself had to live for some time in the shadow of a gas chamber. But also believe me that even then I did not give up my conviction of the unconditional meaningfulness of life, because either life has meaning—and then it retains this meaning even if the life is short lived—or life has no meaning—and then adding ever more years just perpetuates this meaninglessness. And believe me, even a life that has been meaningless all along, that is, a life that has been wasted, may—even in the last moment—still be bestowed with meaning by the very way in which we tackle this situation." And then I told him the story of Leo Tolstoy's *The Death of Ivan Ilyich*—the tale of a man who is about 60 years of age and suddenly learns that he is to die in a couple of days. By the insight he gains from this knowledge and from the realization that he has wasted his life, that his life has been virtually meaningless, he grows beyond himself and finally becomes capable—retro-actively—of flooding his life with infinite meaning.

To all appearances, this message got across. If I had doubted it, I would have been convinced later, when I came across an article in the May 10 *San Francisco Chronicle* about an "unusual press conference" that Aaron Mitchell

began by handing out this brief statement he had typed himself: "I have made my appeal to God and to the Governor. This is my last appeal to Man. Forgive me, for I knew not." As he met newspaper reporters at the prison under the careful eyes of guards, Mitchell said, "I don't really expect clemency from the Governor and I sympathize with him. He will be under criticism either way, but much lighter criticism if he fails to act for me." The condemned man, seemingly much calmer than his interviewers, also said he feared his own execution may start "a long new line to the gas chamber." Mitchell acknowledged the drizzle of rain outside: "It always seems to rain when things are bad, and the rain is God in anger." The first friends he ever had in his life, he said, were two Death Row guards who appeared at his sentence-determining penalty trial after he had been waiting in the prison. "It was the first time in my entire life someone was willing to stand up and say I know this man,

I'll speak in his behalf," Mitchell told reporters. "What I'd like to feel, these last days I have of life, is that if you're home, or in the office, at work or play when you read this, stand up and say to yourself, I feel as if I know this man. He could have been my friend. Because I feel the need of friends in my dying hour," he said.

We must not overlook and forget that even self-administered logotherapy may be helpful, and may even change the life of professionals. In this context, I would like to quote from two letters I recently received:

> All of my life I have been in engineering management. I am presently in a salary bracket which puts me in the upper 2 percent of salaries earned in the United States. Yet in spite of my relatively high salary and the responsible positions I have held I felt an emptiness in my life. It has only been in the last few years that my life started to have meaning. Logotherapy clearly put my life in perspective and allowed me to gain an understanding which I had never had before. I am now in the process of changing my profession from engineering management to clinical psychology. I will not make as much money or be in as responsible a position as I am now in, but I know that the direction I have taken will have more meaning for me regardless of money or position.

Here the frustrated will to meaning had been compensated by the will to power ("position") plus what one might call a "will to money." The man had belonged with those who have the means—the financial means—but no meaning. However, once his will to meaning had been reawakened and meaning began to dawn on him, any overconcern with money (which is the mere means to an end rather than the end itself) subsided. And here is the second letter:

> As a therapist I was primarily Freudian by training. All that Freudian philosophy had promised, I had received in abundance—a very expensive home with pool, two late-model

cars, three healthy, bright children, loving wife and companion and an occupation that brought pride and acceptance from the community—but still something was missing. I felt the existential vacuum. I had accepted the tranquil state as being the end result of therapy. Now that I have reestablished a new quest in my life, the existential vacuum is dissipating. I face surgery of the esophagus and stomach within the next two months. Instead of depression I find myself facing this with the feeling that the experience will make me a better person. The forced loss of thirty-five pounds will certainly be part of this.

Here, as we see, the rediscovery of meaning even included attitudinal values.

That meaning can be found not only in spite of, but also because of, unavoidable suffering, such as an incurable disease—say, an inoperable cancer—is a possibility more easily understood by the man in the street than by the expert in the field. Beverly Hills realtor Fred Harris had inoperable cancer of both lungs. According to a report published in *Time* magazine for August 14, 1972, Harris formed a self-help program through which cancer victims who have more or less adjusted to their illness counsel others who have not. Judd Marmor rightly commented that the project "can also be therapeutic for the person who is doing the helping. It gives him a purpose in life at a point where the curtain seems to be drawing down."[73]

Other authors, however, are not prepared to take such a motivation at its face value. In *Life-Threatening Behavior*, the official journal of the American Association of Suicidology, Paul H. Blachly, of the University of Oregon Medical School, once suggested that the suicidal person who wants to destroy his whole body may find an alternative in sacrificing just a part of it, by donating either blood or an organ to a person who needs it to live. One would assume that Blachly advocates an approach similar to logotherapy, which teaches that suicide may be caused by a feeling of meaninglessness and that its prevention accordingly presupposes that the patient discover a meaning to life. However, this is not so. Blachly apparently does not see man as a being in search of meaning. He therefore cannot understand either that man is willing to sacrifice everything if there is meaning in such a sacrifice, or, the corollary of this proposition, that man does not care for a life without meaning. Once we eliminate from our vision of man the human dimension in which such human phenomena as the will to meaning are located, we must construct, not to say invent, drives and instincts to explain "human" behavior—without recognizing that by the very nature of such an explanation man's behavior actually is dehumanized. Small wonder that Blachly is compelled to hypothesize a "death wish," and believes that a patient who is prone to suicide is a plaything of the death wish. To be sure, this wish "might be purged if the donor gives an organ that is not essential to his own life. People who donate a kidney," Blachly notes, "often experience a sustained feeling of satisfaction"—satisfaction of the death wish, that is.[74] In actual fact, I would say, these people have discovered a meaning to life and a reason for survival. However, a psychology that a priori shuts out meaning and reason cannot recognize the self-transcendent quality of the human reality and instead must resort to drives and instincts. Whenever the pulling force exerted by meanings and reasons is obscured, the pushing force of drives and instincts is hypothesized.[75]

Before, I spoke of meaningful suffering in terms of sacrifice, which brings to mind a story that, because of its brevity, I like to tell my students in order to illustrate how suffering may be bestowed with meaning. It is the story of a physician who suffered from severe depression after his wife died. I embarked on a short Socratic dialogue by asking him what would have happened if he had died first. "How much she would have suffered," he answered. What was now left to me was simply to respond, "Your wife has been spared this suffering, and after all, it is you who are sparing her this suffering—to be sure, at the price that now you have to survive and mourn her." At the same moment, he could see a meaning in his suffering, the meaning of a sacrifice. There was still suffering, but no longer despair. Because *despair is suffering without meaning.*

When I tell this brief story I am; often blamed for having "imposed" meanings and values on the patient. As it happens, however, it can be shown that what I actually did was intuitively elicit from the patient what "the man in the street" knows by virtue of the "wisdom of the heart." Edwin S. Shneidman provided clear-cut "empirical data" relevant to the issue at hand. He distributed to the students at Harvard a class question-naire that included the question, "If and when you are married, would you prefer to outlive your spouse or would you prefer your spouse to outlive you?" The typical male response was in fact to choose to die after the wife.

As an interlude, let us imagine what help could have been offered to the physician whose wife had died if a rigidly orthodox behavior therapist had had to tackle the situation. Let us see what behavior modifiers suggest "when death or some other irrevocable happening deprives one of something cherished. . . . A schedule should be devised by which the individual's efforts are systematically rewarded, sometimes starting with such minor accom-plishments as making a telephone call, mowing the lawn, or washing dishes. These behaviors are praised and in other ways rewarded by the therapist, and after a time come to give the patient a sense of satisfaction quite directly."[76] Let us hope.

As to the feeling of meaninglessness per se, it is an existential despair and a spiritual distress rather than an emotional disease or a mental illness. This, however, in no way implies that we must discard and abolish the medical model. What we must do is simply recognize its limits. Within these limits, mental illness is no "myth" at all, but we have to distinguish among the various levels at which its etiological point of departure may be located. Mental illness may be psychogenic (neurosis) or somatogenic (psychosis) in nature and origin. But noögenic and (psych-) iatrogenic (pseudo-) neuroses also exist. And, last but not least, the existential vacuum exists. It is something sociogenic and not at all a neurosis.

It is important that this be conveyed to the "non-patients" suffering from it. They should know that despair over the apparent meaninglessness of life constitutes a human achievement rather than a neurosis. After all, no animal cares whether or not its existence has a meaning. It is the prerogative of man to quest for a meaning to his life, and also to question whether such meaning exists. This quest is a manifestation of intellectual sincerity and honesty. In particular, it is the challenge of youth to question the meaning of life. However, the courage to question should be matched by patience. People should be patient enough to wait until, sooner or later, meaning dawns on them. This is what they should do, rather than taking their lives—or taking refuge in drugs.

All this should be conveyed to man by way of "first aid" in cases of existential vacuum. To demonstrate how important such first aid might be, I would like to quote Albert Einstein: "The man who regards his life as meaningless is not merely unhappy but hardly fit for life." Indeed, survival is dependent on direction. However, survival cannot be the supreme value. Unless life points to something beyond itself, survival is pointless and meaningless. It is not even possible. This is the very lesson I learned in three years spent in Auschwitz and Dachau, and in the meantime it has been confirmed by psychiatrists in prisoner-of-war camps: Only those who were oriented toward the future, toward a goal in the future, toward a meaning to fulfill in the future, were likely to survive.

And I think that this is not only true of the survival of individuals but also holds for the survival of mankind. For there is hope for mankind's survival only as long as people will arrive at the awareness of common denominators in axiological terms—that is to say, common denominators in what they feel makes their lives worth living. It is thus obvious that the subject boils down to an axiological issue: Will there be values and meanings that can be shared by people—and peoples? Values and meanings they might have in common?

The only thing I know for sure is that if common values and meanings are to be found, another step now must be taken, thousands of years after mankind developed monotheism, the belief in the one God. Monotheism is not enough; it will not do. What we need is not only the belief in the one God but also the awareness of the one mankind, the awareness of the unity of humanity. I would call it "mon-anthropism."

There is survival value in the will to meaning, as we have seen; but as to mankind, there is hope for survival only if mankind is united by a *common* will to a *common* meaning—in other words, by an awareness of common tasks. In the paper quoted previously, Carolyn Wood Sherif reported the results of experiments with children in whom group aggressions had been built up. However, once they were united by the common task of dragging a carriage out of the mud, the kids "forgot" to live out their group aggressions. Let us learn the lesson.

Yet we psychiatrists should refrain from dabbling in fields other than our own. I would say that each issue deserves to be taken up by a specialist. So why not leave something, say, to the sociologists? We psychiatrists simply don't have the answer for each and every question. Least of all do we have a prescription to hand out when it comes to the question of how to cure all the ills that afflict our society. *Let us start humanizing psychiatry rather than divinizing it,* and, to begin with, let us stop ascribing divine attributes to psychiatrists. We psychiatrists are neither omniscient nor omnipotent, we are only omnipresent: mingling at all symposia, and joining in all discussions . . .

As to logotherapy, it is not a panacea.[77] It therefore is open to cooperation with other approaches to psychotherapy; it is open to its own evolution; and it is open to religion. This is indispensable. It is true, logotherapy deals with the *logos*; it deals with meaning. Specifically, I see the meaning of logotherapy in helping others to see meaning in life. But one cannot "give" meaning to the life of others. And if this is true of meaning per se, how much more does it hold for ultimate meaning? *The more comprehensive the meaning, the less comprehensible it is.* Infinite meaning is necessarily beyond the comprehension of a finite being. Here is the point at which science gives up and wisdom takes over.

Wisdom is knowledge plus: knowledge—and the knowledge of its own limits.

CHAPTER 9

Man's Search for Ultimate Meaning*

Ladies and gentlemen,

If a speaker comes from Vienna you certainly expect him to speak with a heavy Viennese accent—as I do; and if he is a psychiatrist, at that, you also expect him to start his lecture with a reference to Sigmund Freud—why not:

All of us have learned from him to see in man a being basically concerned with seeking pleasure. It was Freud, after all, who introduced the concept of the *pleasure principle,* and the coexistence of the reality principle does in no way contradict his hypothesis of seeking pleasure as man's primary motivation; for, as he repeatedly stated, the reality principle is a mere extension of the pleasure principle, still serving the latter's purpose, which remains: pleasure "and nothing but pleasure."

But we must not overlook and forget that the pleasure principle itself is—also according to Freud—no more than the servant of a more comprehensive principle, namely, of the *homeostasis principle* (Cannon, 1932), whose

---

* Oskar Pfister Award Lecture 1985 at the Annual Meeting of the American Psychiatric Association in Dallas, Texas.

goal is tension reduction for the sake of maintaining, or restoring, the inner equilibrium.

However, what is missing in the frame of such an image of man is that fundamental characteristic of the human reality which I have come to term its *self-transcendent* quality. I thereby want to denote the intrinsic fact that being human always relates and points to something other than itself—better to say, something or *someone*. That is to say, rather than being concerned with any inner condition, be it pleasure or homeostasis, man is oriented toward the world out there, and within this world, he is interested in meanings to fulfill, and in other human beings. By virtue of what I would call the pre-reflective ontological self-understanding he knows that he is actualizing himself precisely to the extent to which he is forgetting himself, and he is forgetting himself by giving himself, be it through serving a cause higher than himself, or loving a person other than himself. Truly, self-transcendence is the essence of human existence.

It would seem that also the second of the two classic schools of Viennese psychotherapy—Adlerian psychology—does not pay sufficient tribute to self-transcendence. It mainly considers man a being who is out to overcome a certain inner condition, namely, the feeling of inferiority which he tries to get rid of by developing the striving for superiority—a concept that is by and large congruent with the Nietzschean will to power.

As long as a motivation theory pivots on the "will to pleasure," as we could rename the Freudian pleasure principle, or on the Adlerian striving for superiority, it proves to be a typical representative of so-called "depth psychology." But what about a "height psychology" (Frankl, 1938) which takes into account the so-called "higher aspirations" of the human psyche: not only man's seeking pleasure and power but also his search for meaning. It was Oskar Pfister (1904) who recommended to

move in such a direction when he as early as in 1904!—
pointed out that "more important" (sc. in comparison with
depth psychology) "is the recognition of that spiritual
height of our nature which is as powerful as its instinctual
depth."

It is true, rather than being a substitute for depth
psychology, height psychology is only a supplement (to be
sure, a necessary one); but it does focus on the specifically
human phenomena—among them man's desire to find and
fulfill a meaning in his life, or for that matter in the
individual life situations confronting him. I have circumscribed this most human of all human needs by the
motivation theoretical term *will to meaning* (Frankl, 1949).

Today, man's will to meaning is frustrated on a
worldwide scale. Ever more people are haunted by a
feeling of meaninglessness which is often accompanied by
a feeling of emptiness—or, as I am used to calling it, an
"existential vacuum" (Frankl, 1955). It mainly manifests
itself in boredom and apathy. While boredom is indicative
of a loss of interest in the world, apathy betrays a lack of
the initiative to do something in the world, to change
something in the world.

So much for the phenomenology of the existential
vacuum. And what about its epidemiology? Let me
restrict myself to randomly picking up a passage that
you may find in a book authored by Irvin D. Yalom (1980):
"Of forty consecutive patients applying for therapy at a
psychiatric outpatient clinic, 30 percent had some major
problem involving meaning as adjudged from self-
ratings, therapists, or independent judges." As to myself,
I neither think that each and every case of neurosis, let
alone of psychosis, is to be traced back to a feeling of
meaninglessness, nor do I think that a feeling of
meaninglessness necessarily results in mental illness. In
other words, neither is each and every case of neurosis
"noögenic" (Frankl, 1959), i.e., deriving from an existential

vacuum; nor is, conversely, the existential vacuum in each and every case pathogenic. Even less is it anything pathological. I rather regard it as a prerogative and privilege of man not only to quest for a meaning to his life but also to question whether such a meaning exists at all. No other animal asks such a question, not even one of Konrad Lorenz' clever grey geese does so; but man does.

In a way, the existential vacuum may well be considered a sociogenic neurosis. No doubt, our industrialized society is out to satisfy all human needs, and its companion, consumer society, is even out to create ever new needs to satisfy; but the most human need—the need to find and fulfill a meaning in our lives—is frustrated by this society. In the wake of industrialization, urbanization tends to uproot man from traditions and to alienate him from those values which are transmitted by the traditions. Understandably, it is in particular the young generation who is most affected by the resulting feeling of meaninglessness, as could be evidenced by empirical research. More specifically, such phenomena as addiction, aggression, and depression are, in the final analysis, due to a sense of futility. Again to restrict myself to one quotation: Of the drug addicts studied by Stanley Krippner, "things seemed meaningless" to not less than 100 percent.

But after all these glimpses into the pathology of the *Zeitgeist* it is now time to ask ourselves, What is meant by meaning? Well, this word is used here in a sense that is absolutely "down to earth" inasmuch as it refers to that which a concrete situation means to a concrete person. And as to the cognition of meaning, I would say, it is to be located midway between a Gestalt perception, say, along the lines of Max Wertheimer's theory, and an "aha experience" along the lines of Karl Buhler's concept. Kurt Lewin as well as Max Wertheimer (1961) spoke of "demand characteristics" and "demand qualities," respectively, as they are inherent in a given situation. In fact, each life situation confronting us places a demand on us, presents a question to us—a question to which we have to answer by doing something about the given situation. Thus, the perception of meaning differs from the classical concept of Gestalt perception insofar as the latter boils down to suddenly becoming aware of a "figure" on a "ground," whereas the perception of meaning, as I see it, could be defined as suddenly becoming aware of a possibility against the background of reality.

It goes without saying that we psychiatrists cannot tell a patient what a situation should mean to him. Even less is it possible to tell him wherein he should see the meaning of his life as a whole. But we may well show him that life never ceases to offer us a meaning up to its last moment, up to our last breath. We are indebted to no less than 20 researchers for—on strictly empirical grounds!—having convinced us that people are capable of finding meaning in their lives irrespective of gender, age, IQ, educational background, character structure, environment, and, most remarkably, also irrespective of whether or not they are religious, and if so, irrespective of the denomination to which they may belong. I thereby refer to the work of Brown, Casciani, Crumbaugh, Dansart, Durlac, Kratochvil, Levinson, Lukas, Lunceford, Mason, Meier, Murphy, Planova, Popielski, Richmond, Roberts, Ruch, Sallee, Smith, Yarnell, and Young (cf. Frankl, 1985a).

From this it follows that there must be a meaning to life under any conditions, even the worst conceivable ones. But how shall we explain this finding which so much contradicts the ubiquitous feeling of meaninglessness? Well, if we investigate how the man in the street goes about finding meaning it turns out that there are three avenues that lead up to meaning fulfillment: First, doing a deed or creating a work; second, experiencing something or encountering someone; in other words, meaning can be found not only in work but also in love. Most important, however, is the third avenue: Facing a fate we cannot change, we are called upon to make the best of it by rising above ourselves and growing beyond ourselves, in a word, by changing ourselves. And this equally holds for the three components of the "tragic triad"—pain, guilt, and death—inasmuch as we may turn suffering into a human achievement and accomplishment; derive from guilt the opportunity to change for the better; and see in life's transitoriness an incentive to take responsible action (Frankl, 1984a).

As to suffering, let me quote from the book of a German bishop (Moser, 1978) the following incident:

> A few years after World War II a doctor examined a Jewish woman who wore a bracelet made of baby teeth mounted in gold. "A beautiful bracelet," the doctor remarked. "Yes," the woman answered, "this tooth here belonged to Miriam, this one to Esther, and this one to Samuel. . . ." She mentioned the names of her daughters and sons according to age. "Nine children," she added, "and all of them were taken to the gas chambers." Shocked, the doctor asked: "How can you live with such a bracelet?" Quietly, the Jewish woman replied: "I am now in charge of an orphanage in Israel."

As you see, meaning may be squeezed out even from suffering, and that is the very reason why life remains potentially meaningful in spite of everything. But is this to say that suffering is indispensable for finding a meaning to life? In no way. I only insist that meaning is available in spite of—nay, even through—suffering, provided, to be sure, that we have to deal with unavoidable suffering. If it were avoidable, the meaningful thing to do would be to remove its cause, be it psychological, biological, or sociological. Unnecessary suffering would be masochistic rather than heroic.

When setting out to discuss the meaning of meaning I referred to meaning as something "down to earth." However, it cannot be denied that there is also some sort of meaning that is "up to heaven," as it were; some sort of ultimate meaning, that is; a meaning of the whole, of the "universe," or at least a meaning of one's life as a whole; at any rate, a long-range meaning. And I do not think that it is worthy of a psychiatrist—or, for that matter, of any scientist—to deny on a priori grounds that such a long-range meaning does exist. To invoke an analogy, consider a movie: It consists of thousands upon thousands of individual pictures, and each of them makes sense and carries a meaning, yet the meaning of the whole film cannot be seen before its last sequence is shown. On the other hand, we cannot understand the whole film without having first understood each of its components, each of the individual pictures. Isn't it the same with life? Doesn't the final meaning of life, too, reveal itself, if ever at all, only at its end, on the verge of death? And doesn't the final meaning, too, depend on whether or not the potential meaning of each single situation has been actualized to the best of the respective individual's knowledge and belief?

But once that we start dealing with an overall meaning we soon meet a law that I would like to formulate as follows: *The more comprehensive the meaning, the less comprehensible it is.* And if it comes to *ultimate meaning,* also, it necessarily is beyond comprehension. "Consider a poor dog whom they are vivisecting in a laboratory," William James (1897) said, when addressing the Harvard Young Men's Christian Association:

> He cannot see a single redeeming ray in the whole business; and yet all these diabolic-seeming events are often controlled by human intentions with which, if his poor benighted mind could only be made to catch a glimpse of them, all that is heroic in him would religiously acquiesce. Lying on his back on the board there he may be performing a function incalculably higher than any that prosperous canine life admits of; and yet, of the whole performance, this function is the one portion that must remain absolutely beyond his ken. Now turn from this to the life of man. Although we only see our world, and the dog's

within it, yet encompassing both these worlds a still wider world may be there, as unseen by us as our world is by him.

What William James here did is, I would say, some sort of extrapolation. Well, I pride myself of having done something parallel—without knowing of James's priority—when I once stepped into a room of my hospital department where a doctor on my staff was conducting a psychodrama. The mother of a boy who had died at the age of 11 years had been admitted after a suicide attempt. Now she was telling her story:

> At the death of her boy she was left alone with another, older son, who was severely handicapped. The poor boy had to be moved around in a wheelchair. His mother rebelled—against her fate. But when she tried to commit suicide together with him, it was the son who prevented her from doing so; he liked living! For him, life had remained meaningful despite the handicap. Why was it not so for his mother? How could her life still have a meaning? And how could we help her to become aware of it? Improvising, I participated in the discussion, and addressing myself to the whole group, I asked the patients whether an ape which was being used to develop poliomyelitis serum, and for this reason punctured again and again, would ever be able to grasp the meaning of its suffering. Unanimously, the group replied that of course it would not; with its limited intelligence, it could not enter into the world of man, i.e., the only world in which the meaning of its suffering would be understandable. Then I pushed forward with the following question: "And what about man? Are you sure that the human world is a terminal point in the evolution of the cosmos? Is it not conceivable that there is still another dimension, a world beyond man's world; a world in which the question of an ultimate meaning of human suffering would find an answer?" (Frankl, 1984a)

I just referred to "another dimension," at the same time indicating that it would not be accessible to reason or intellect. By the same token, it necessarily would elude any strictly scientific approach. Small wonder that ultimate meaning is missing in the world as described by science. However, does this imply that the world is *void* of ultimate meaning? I think it only shows that science is *blind* to ultimate meaning. Ultimate meaning is scotomized by science. However, this state of affairs does in no way entitle a scientist to deny that ultimate meaning possibly does exist. It is perfectly legitimate that the scientist as such restricts himself to a certain "cross section" he cuts through reality, and it may well happen that within this cross section no meaning whatsoever can be found. But he should remain aware that also other cross sections are conceivable.

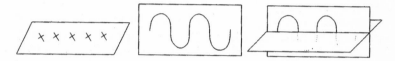

Consider a horizontal plane wherein five points are located—isolated points, disconnected points, points without a meaningful connection between them. Well, these points should serve as symbols for events that, at least at first sight, seem to be "pure chance, only chance," to apply the words used by Jacques Monod in his book *Chance and Necessity* when he spoke of those mutations which account for no more or less than evolution: He conceived of them as random events, that is to say, events with no meaning behind them. But what about having a vertical plane orthogonally intersect the horizontal one in such a way that the five points prove to be the spots on which a curve lying in the vertical plane intersects the horizontal one—suddenly we become aware that there does exist a connection between the five points although it hides in a different dimension. Well, isn't it possible that there also exists a meaningful connection between what, at first sight, seems to be no more than random events such as the mutations? Once we no longer keep our view restricted to the biological plane but widen our horizon by including in our view the next higher dimension we immediately recognize that here, too, a "higher" or "deeper" meaning may well exist although it does not show up in the lower dimension—exactly as the "higher" or the "lower" portions of the curve were not discernible on the horizontal plane.

The fact remains that not everything can be explained in meaningful terms. But what now can be explained is at least the reason why this is *necessarily* impossible. At least it is impossible on merely intellectual grounds. An irrational rest is left. But what is "unknowable" need not be unbelievable. In fact, where knowledge gives up, the torch is passed on to faith. True, it is not possible to find out intellectually whether everything is ultimately meaningless or whether there is ultimate meaning behind everything. But if we cannot answer the question intellectually we may well do so existentially. Where an intellectual cognition fails an existential decision is due. Vis-à-vis the fact that it is equally conceivable that everything is absolutely meaningful and that everything is absolutely meaningless, in other words, that the scales are equally high, we must throw the weight of our own being into one of the scales. And precisely therein I see the function to carry out my belief. In contrast to what people are prone to assume, namely, believing is not at all some sort of thinking *minus* the *reality* of that which is thought, believing is rather some sort of thinking *plus* something, namely, the *existentiality* of him or her who does the thinking.

And how does the man, or the woman, in the street actually proceed in the face of the "unknowable," or let me, in order to answer this question, ask you another one: Did you ever stand on a stage? If so, you may remember that, blinded by footlights and spotlights, you saw in front of yourself just a "black hole" rather than anything such as an audience. But you still remained "believing" in the existence and presence of the audience, didn't you? Well, the same holds for a portion of the human population on our planet, however large or small the portion may be; they, too, remain believing. . . . Blinded by the trivialities of everyday life, they fill the "black hole" with symbols. Like the actor, or the actress, who cannot see the audience before which they play their roles—likewise human beings desire to read into, to project into, to "see into" the nothing confronting them—a something or, better to say, a someone. To put it in a joking vein, they espouse that nuclear tenet of existentialism which I would like to epitomize as follows: Nothingness is really nothingness. That is to say, an ultimate being—paralleling the ultimate meaning—or, to speak in plain words, God, is not one thing among others but being itself or Being (capitalized by Martin Heidegger). From this it follows that you cannot simply place the ultimate being on the same plane as things unless you wish to succumb to the same fallacy as a little boy once did when he told my wife that he knew what he was going to be when he grew up. She asked what it would be and he answered, "Either I'll be an acrobat on a trapeze in a circus or I'll be God." He dealt with God as if being God were one vocation among other vocations (Frankl, 1984b).

Particularly in context with the ultimate being the gap, nay, the abyss between that which is to *symbolize* on one hand and on the other hand that which is to be symbolized, becomes painful. But to dismiss, or renounce, symbolization because a symbol is never indentical with that for which it stands is unwarranted. Just consider a painting that shows, above a landscape, the sky: Any painter who is a representative of realism more often than not induces the onlooker to "see" the sky by putting a couple of clouds thereon. But are not the clouds precisely something that is not-identical with the sky? Isn't it true that they rather hide it, preventing us from seeing it? Still, the clouds serve as the best and simplest symbol for the sky, don't they?

By and large, the divine, too, is symbolized by what it is not: Its attributes are *human* properties, not to say all too human ones. God is portrayed in a more or less anthropomorphic way and manner. And yet we are not justified in discarding religion solely on account of all its anthropomorphic ingredients. Asymptotically approaching the enigma of ultimate truth on the symbolic rather than on an abstract level may eventually yield a more productive result. Believe it or not, it was Konrad Lorenz (1981) who improvisingly said—in a recent conversation with Franz Kreuzer—"If you compare the validity of the worldview *(Weltanschauung)* of an alpine farmer's wife with the validity of B. F. Skinner's worldview you discover that the farmer's wife who believes in the immaculate conception of the Holy Mary, in the Dear Lord, and in all the Saints still has come closer to truth than the behaviorist."

On the other hand, there are undeniable pitfalls in store for us whenever we embark on anthropomorphism uncritically. An instance that illustrates the point is the following joke: A Sunday school teacher once told her class a story of a poor man whose wife had died in childbirth. He could not afford to hire a wet nurse, but God worked a miracle by letting breasts grow on the chest of the poor man so that the newborn baby could be suckled. One of the boys, however, objected that there was no need to work a miracle. Why did not God simply arrange for the poor man to find an envelope with a thousand dollars to pay a wet nurse? But the teacher replied: "You are a silly boy. If God can work a miracle he certainly will not throw away cash." Why do we laugh? Because a certain human category, namely, saving cash, has been applied to the motivations of God (Frankl, 1984b).

After discussing the need for symbols we may define religion as a system of symbols, i.e., symbols for that which humans cannot grasp in conceptual terms. But isn't the need for symbols, the capacity to create them and to use them, a fundamental characteristic of being human at large? Isn't the capacity to speak and to understand speech acknowledged as a distinctive feature of humanness? Well, it is also legitimate to define the individual languages developed by mankind as "systems of symbols." But comparing religion with language one should also keep in mind that nobody is justified in claiming that the particular language spoken by himself is superior to another one. After all, it is possible in any language to arrive at truth—at the one truth—and it is also possible in any language to err and to lie.

However, we are not only confronted with linguistic pluralism but also with religious pluralism, the latter being represented by the fact that, by and large, religion is split up in various denominations. And, again, one denomination cannot claim superiority over or against another. But isn't it conceivable that, sooner or later, religious pluralism will be overcome and replaced by religious universalism? I do not think so. I do not deem it probable that some sort of a religious Esperanto could ever serve as a substitute for the individual denominations. What is looming is not a universal religion but rather the contrary: If religion is to survive it will have to become a profoundly personalized religion which allows any human being to speak a language of his or her own when addressing himself or herself to the ultimate being.*

Is this to imply that the individual denominations or for that matter the respective organizations and institutions will fade away? Not necessarily. For—however different the personal styles may be in which human beings express

* Gordon W. Allport, in his renowned book, *The Individual and His Religion,* refers to profoundly personalized religion when he speaks of the Hindu religion. (Allport, 1956).

their search for an ultimate meaning and/or address themselves to an ultimate being—there are, and always will be, symbols that are common to communities. Or aren't there languages that—despite their differences—have the same alphabet in common?

I admit that the concept of religion in its widest possible sense as it is here propounded goes far beyond the narrow concepts of God as they are promulgated by some representatives of denominational religion. They often depict, not to say denigrate, God as a being who is primarily concerned with being believed in by the greatest possible number of believers and along the lines of a specific creed, at that. "Just believe," we are told, "and everything will be okay." But alas, not only is this order based on a distortion of any sound concept of deity, but even more important, it is doomed to failure: Obviously, there are certain activities that simply cannot be commanded, demanded, or ordered. You cannot order anyone to laugh— if you want him to laugh, you must tell him a joke. And if you want people to have faith and belief in God, you cannot rely on preaching along the lines of a particular church but must, in the first place, portray your God believably—and you must act credibly yourself. In other words, you have to do the very opposite of what so often is done by the representatives of organized religion when they build up an image of God as someone who is primarily interested in being believed in and who rigorously insists that those who believe in him be affiliated with a particular church. Small wonder that such representatives of religion behave as though they saw the main task of their own denomination as that of overriding other denominations.

Before, we spoke of addressing oneself to deity in an utmost personal mode of expression: Usually, such a mode of speaking to God is called praying. Truly, prayer is a "person-to-person call." Indeed, it could be considered the climax of the "I–Thou" relationship that Martin Buber regarded as the most characteristic quality of human existence, that is, its dialogical quality. However, I think that there are not only interpersonal but also intrapersonal dialogues, inner dialogues, dialogues within ourselves. In other words, dialogues need not take place between an *ego* and a *tu* but may take place between an *ego* and an *alter ego* as well. And it is in this context that I would like to offer you a peculiar definition of God at which, I confess, I arrived at the age of 15 years. In a sense, it is an operational definition. It reads as follows: God is the partner of our most intimate soliloquies. That is to say, whenever you are talking to yourself in utmost sincerity and ultimate solitude—he to whom you are addressing yourself may justifiably be called God. As you notice, such a definition circumvents the bifurcation between atheistic and theistic *Weltanschauung*. The difference between them emerges only later on, when the irreligious person insists that his soliloquies are just that, monologues with himself, and the religious person interprets his as real dialogues with someone other than himself. Well, I think that what here should count first and more than anything else is the "utmost sincerity" and honesty. And I am sure that if God really exists he certainly is not going to argue with the irreligious persons because they mistake him for their own selves and therefore misname him.

The question still remains whether "irreligious persons" really exist. In a book of mine, *The Unconscious God*, I assemble and evaluate some indications to the effect that a religious sense is existent and present in each and every person, albeit buried, not to say repressed, in the unconscious (Frankl, 1985a). In other words, when Freud once contended that man is "not only often much more immoral that he believes, but also often much more moral than he thinks," we may say that he is often much more religious than he admits. This omnipresence of religion (to be sure, "religion" in its widest possible sense), its ubiquity in the unconscious, may well account for the fact (already discussed) that—as empirically evidenced by tests and statistics—people who regard themselves as irreligious are no less capable of finding meaning in their lives than those who consider themselves to be religious.

Small wonder that such an inherent (though inexplicit) religiousness proves to be more persistent and resistant than we may expect it to be inasmuch as it defies outer as well as inner circumstances to an incredible degree. Once, for example, I had the doctors of my hospital department screen an unselected group of patients regarding the correlation of their father image with their religious development. It turned out that a poor religious life cannot simply be traced back to the impact of a negative father image. Nor does even the worst father image necessarily prevent one from establishing a sound religious *Weltanschauung* (Frankl, 1985b).

So much regarding the impact of education. How about the environment's influence? Suffice it to point out that—as far as both my professional experience (Frankl, 1985c) and my personal experiences (Frankl, 1986) offer evidence—religion did not even die in Auschwitz, nor "after Auschwitz," to allude to the title of a book that was authored by a rabbi (who incidentally had not been there). I personally think that either belief in God is unconditional or it is not belief at all. If it is unconditional it will stand and face the fact that six million died in the Nazi holocaust; if it is not unconditional it will fall away if only a single innocent child has to die—to resort to an argument once advanced by Dostoyevski.

The truth is that among those who actually went through the experience of Auschwitz, the number of those whose religious life was deepened—in spite, not to say because, of this experience—by far exceeds the number of those who gave up their belief. To paraphrase what La Rochefoucauld once remarked with regard to the effect that separation has on love, one might say that just as the small fire is extinguished by the storm while a large fire is enhanced by it—likewise a weak faith is weakened by predicaments and catastrophes whereas a strong faith is strengthened by them.

So much for the outer circumstances. And what about the inner ones? For instance, psychoses? In a book of mine, *The Will to Meaning,* I describe the case of a severe manic phase (Frankl, 1984b), in other books of mine a patient suffering from an endogenous depression (Frankl, 1985a) and other patients suffering from schizophrenia (Frankl, 1984a,b)—all of them showed an indestructible and indelible sense of religiousness.

Ladies and gentlemen, after propounding an operational definition of religion as impartial and neutral as mine—encompassing even agnosticism and atheism—I hope to be justified in contending (1) that I was entitled, indeed, to deal with religion as a psychiatrist and (2) that I also remained a psychiatrist throughout my presentation by treating religion as a *human* phenomenon, more specifically, as an outgrowth of what I regard to be the most human of all human phenomena, namely, the "will to meaning." Religion, we may say, revealed itself as the fulfillment of what we now may call the *"will to ultimate meaning."*

Incidentally, my definition of religion is paralleled by another one which was presented by Albert Einstein (1950) and reads as follows: "To be religious is to have found an answer to the question, What is the meaning of life?" And there is still another definition which was offered by Ludwig Wittgenstein (1960) and reads as follows: "To believe in God is to see that life has a meaning." As you see, Einstein, the physicist, and Wittgenstein, the philosopher, as well as I myself as a psychiatrist arrived at definitions of religion that are overlapping each other.

To be sure, there is a question to be left open or, better to say, to be answered by the theologian, namely the question: To which extent are the three definitions of religion acceptable to him? The only thing we psychiatrists can do is to keep the dialogue between religion and psychiatry going; going on in the spirit of that mutual tolerance which is indispensable in the era of pluralism and in the area of medicine; but also in the spirit of that mutual tolerance which imbues the memorable exchange of letters between Oskar Pfister and Sigmund Freud.

Thank you for your attention.

Notes

Chapter 1

1. Sigmund Freud, *Three Essays on the Theory of Sexuality* (London: Image, 1949).
2. Cf. Viktor E. Frankl, "Zur geistigen Problematik der Psychotherapie," *Zentralblatt für Psychotherapie,* 10,33 (1938). Viktor E. Frankl, "Philosophie und Psychotherapie. Zur Grundlegung einer Existenzanalyse," *Schweizerische medizinische Wochenschrift,* 69, 707 (1939).
3. The English version is *The Doctor and the Soul: From Psychotherapy to Logotherapy* (New York: Alfred A. Knopf, Inc., 1965).

Chapter 2

1. Cf. Friedrich von Schiller's epigram, *"Spricht die Seele, so spricht, ach, schon die Seele nicht mehr,"* which means, "As soon as the soul starts talking, it is no longer the soul who is talking." Likewise, we might say that once the self reflects on itself, it is no longer the true self that exhibits itself.

Chapter 3

1. See Viktor E. Frankl, *Psychotherapy and Existentialism: Selected Papers on Logotherapy* (New York: Washington Square Press, 1967; Touchstone paperback, 1968).

Chapter 6

1. Viktor E. Frankl, *The Doctor and the Soul: From Psychotherapy to Logotherapy* (New York: Alfred A. Knopf, Inc.; second, expanded edition, 1965; paperback edition, New York: Vintage Books, 1973). The original (German) version was published in 1946.
2. Quoted from *Psychologie und Religion,* our translation.
3. In my book *The Will to Meaning* I have expressed my conviction that there is a dimensional barrier between the human world and the divine world, a barrier that prevents man from really speaking of God. He "cannot speak of God but he may speak to God. He may pray," I have said in this context. It is noteworthy, however, that a full awareness of this insurmountable inadequacy of the God concept can, as it were, be built in in a prayer, forming part of its contents. For an example, I may refer to the Hebrew prayer for the dead, Kaddish, more specifically, a passage to the effect that God is "high above all the blessings and hymns, praises and consolations which are uttered in the world."
4. Much of what is derogatively called "organized religion" rather deserves the name "organic religion" because it has grown organically instead of being fabricated and propagated as ideologies are.

Chapter 8

1. Viktor E. Frankl, "Beyond Self-Actualization and Self-Expression," *Journal of Existential Psychiatry,* 1, 1 (Spring, I960), pp. 5–20.

2. Abraham H. Maslow, *Eupsychian Management* (Homewood, I11: Irwin, 1965).
3. Personal communication from Professor Orlo Strunk, Jr.
4. Psychometric Affiliates, P.O. Box 3167, Munster, Indiana 46321.
5. Abraham H. Maslow, "Comments on Dr. Frankl's Paper," in Anthony J. Sutich and Miles A. Vich, eds., *Readings in Humanistic Psychology* (New York: The Free Press, 1969).
6. Robert L. Jacobson, *The Chronicle of Higher Education* (Washington, DC: American Council on Education, January 10, 1972).
7. *Los Angeles Times,* February 12, 1971.
8. Maslow's hierarchy of needs is also disproved by empiry in the widest possible sense: Consider the living conditions, say, in Auschwitz—can you imagine a situation more insecure regarding one's survival? And yet, in spite of all the insecurity and improbability of survival under the circumstances, in other words, in spite of the extreme frustration of the need for security, some people did search for, and even find, meaning in the midst of the abyss experience called Auschwitz—and Father Maximilian Kolbe found meaning within the fraction of a second when he decided to sacrifice his life, asking the SS for permission to let himself be sentenced to death instead of a family father. . . .
9. Joseph Katz, in *Psychology Today,* 5,1 (June, 1971).
10. James C. Crumbaugh, "The Validation of Logotherapy," in R. M. Jurjevich, ed., *Direct Psychotherapy* (Coral Gables, Fla: University of Miami Press manuscript, 1973).
11. Z. J. Lipowski, "The Conflict of Buridan's Ass, or Some Dilemmas of Affluence," *The American Journal of Psychiatry,* 127 (1970), pp. 49–55.
12. Elisabeth S. Lukas, Dissertation, University of Vienna, 1970.
13. Albert Schweitzer once said, "The only ones among you who will be really happy are those who have sought and found how to serve."
14. "Paradoxical Intention and De-reflection: Two Logotherapeutic Techniques," in Silvano Arieti and Gerard

Chrzanowski, eds., *New Dimensions in Psychiatry* (New York: Wiley-Interscience, 1975).

15. Sometimes sex is also less than sex. William Simon and John Henry Gagnon contend that Freud went wrong in interpreting the sexuality of children with grown-up eyes. "It is dangerous to assume," the authors write, "that because some childhood behavior appears sexual to adults, it must be sexual." Parents who catch a young child playing with his genital organs will instinctively define the act as masturbation; to the child, the experience may well be a nonsexual experience of bodily discovery (*Time* Magazine, March 28,1969).

16. Robert Athanesiou, Phillip Shaver, and Carlo Tavris, "A *Psychology Today* Report on 20,000 Responses to 101 Questions about Sexual Attitudes and Practices," *Psychology Today*, 4 (1970), pp. 37-52.

17. Once we recognize that uniqueness, personhood and self-hood really are interchangeable terms, we may say that the more one becomes himself, the more human he is. Cf. Viktor E. Frankl, "The Depersonalization of Sex," *Synthesis (The Realization of the Self)*, 1, 1, (Spring 1974), pp. 7–11.

18. Cf. Viktor E. Frankl, "Encounter: The Concept and Its Vulgarization," *The Journal of the American Academy of Psychoanalysis*, 1,1 (1973), pp. 73-83.

19. Louis L. Klitzke, "Students in Emerging Africa: Humanistic Psychology and Logotherapy in Tanzania," *American Journal of Humanistic Psychology*, 9 (1969), pp. 105–126.

20. Osvald Vymetal, *Acta Universitatis Palackiannae*, 13 (1966), pp. 265–288.

21. R. N. Gray *et al.*,"An Analysis of Physicians' Attitudes of Cynicism and Humanitarianism before and after Entering Medical Practice," *Journal of Medical Education*, 40 (1955), p. 760.

22. Joseph Wilder, "Values and Psychotherapy," *American Journal of Psychotherapy*, 23 (1969), p. 405.

23. Julius Heuscher, *Journal of Existentialism*, 5 (1964), p. 229.

24. Edith Weisskopf-Joelson *et al.*, "Relative Emphasis on Nine Values by a Group of College Students," *Psychological Report*, 24 (1969), p. 299.

25. The value that ranks next to self-interpretation is self-actualization. Ultimately, however, man can actualize himself only by fulfilling a meaning out in the world, rather than within himself, and self-actualization is available only as an effect of self-transcendence.

26. Earl A. Grollman, *Concerning Death: A Practical Guide for the Living* (Boston: Beacon Press, 1974).

27. Vann A. Smith, personal communication.

28. Betty Lou Padelford, "The Influence of Ethnic Background, Sex, and Father Image upon the Relationship between Drug Involvement and Purpose in Life" (United States International University, San Diego, January 1973).

29. Reviews of the studies by Nowlis, Judd, *et al.*, Mirin *et al.*, Linn, and Krippner *et al.* can be found in Padelford, "The Influence of Ethnic Background" (see note 32).

30. Glenn D. Shean and Freddie Fechtman, "Purpose of Life Scores of Student Marihuana Users," *Journal of Clinical Psychology* 14 (1972), pp. 112–113.

31. Annemarie Von Forstmeyer, (Ph.D. dissertation, United States International University, San Diego, 1970).

32. James C. Crumbaugh, "Changes in Frankl's Existential Vacuum as a Measure of Therapeutic Outcome," *Newsletter for Research in Psychology*, 14 (1972), pp. 35–37.

33. Carolyn Wood Sherif, "Intergroup Conflict and Competition: Social-Psychological Analysis" (paper presented to Scientific Congress, XX Olympic Games, Munich, August 22, 1972, at plenary session on Sport and Conflict).

34. Fredrick Wertham, *American Journal of Psychotherapy*, 26 (1972), p. 216.

35. Jerome D. Frank, "Some Psychological Determinants of Violence and Its Control," *Australia New Zealand Psychiatry*, 6 (1972), pp. 158-164.

36. Bromley H. Kniveton and Geoffrey M. Stephenson, "An Examination of Individual Susceptibility to the Influence of Aggressive Film Models," *British Journal of Psychiatry* 122, 566 (1973), pp. 53–56.

37. John P. Murray, "Television and Violence," *American Psychologist*, 28 (1973), pp. 472–478.

38. Robert Jay Lifton, *History and Human Survival* (New York: Random House, 1969).
39. W. A. M. Black and R. A. M. Gregson, "Time Perspective, Purpose in Life, Extroversion and Neuroticism in New Zealand Prisoners," *British Journal of Social and Clinical Psychology*, 12 (1973), pp. 50–60.
40. Judd Marmor, "The Current Status of Psychoanalysis in American Psychiatry," *American Journal of Psychiatry*, 125 (1968), pp. 131-132.
41. T. P. Millar, "Who's Afraid of Sigmund Freud?" *British Journal of Psychiatry*, 115 (1969), pp. 421-428.
42. H. J. Eysenck, *Behavior Therapy and the Neuroses* (New York: Pergamon Press, 1960), pp. ix, 4, 13, 82.
43. Viktor E. Frankl, "Zur medikamentosen Unterstützung der Psychotherapie bei Neurosen," *Schweizer Archiv für Neurologie und Psychiatrie*, 43 (1939), 26–31.
44. Viktor E. Frankl, *Die Psychotherapie in der Praxis*, (Vienna: Franz Deuticke, 1947).
45. Christa Kohler, "Der Einfluss des Menschenbildes auf die Neurosentheorie," in L. Pickenhain and A. Thom, eds., *Beiträge zu einer allgemeinen Theorie der Psychiatrie* (Jena: Fischer, 1968).
46. Petrilowitsch really spoke in this context of its having "rehumanized *psychoanalysis.*" In addition to the statement made by Petrilowitsch there is a similar one made by the Norwegian learning theorist and behavior therapist Bjarne Kvilhaug to the effect that "logotherapy has rehumanized *learning theory.*"
47. Iver Hand, (paper read at the Symposium on "Logotherapy: Theory and Practice," sponsored by the American Psychological Association, Montreal, 1973).
48. L. Solyom, J. Garza-Perez, B. L. Ledwidge, and C. Solyom, "Paradoxical Intention in the Treatment of Obsessional Thoughts: A Pilot Study," *Comprehensive Psychiatry*, 13, 3 (May 1972), pp. 291–297. Also see Viktor E. Frankl, "Paradoxical Intention: A Logotherapeutic Technique," in Harold Greenwald, ed., *Active Psychotherapy* (New York: Atherton Press, 1967).
49. Edith Weisskopf-Joelson, "Some Suggestions Concerning

the Concept of Awareness," *Psychotherapy*, 8 (1971), pp. 2–7.

50. Max Wertheimer, "Some Problems in the Theory of Ethics," in M. Henle, ed., *Documents of Gestalt Psychology* (Berkeley: University of California Press, 1961).

51. Crumbaugh, "The Validation of Logotherapy," (see note 14).

52. Zev W. Wanderer, "Existential Depression Treated by Desensitization of Phobias: Strategy and Transcript," *Journal of Behavior Therapy and Experimental Psychiatry*, 3 (1972), pp. 111-116.

53. Gordon W. Allport, "Psychological Models for Guidance," *Harvard Educational Review*, 32 (1962), p. 373.

54. The professor's existential vacuum may be transmitted as well. "If teachers show in their attitudes and actions that they are cynical, bored and defeated, the young will get the message, no matter how many literary classics they are required to read" (Arthur G. Wirth, "New Directions in Schools," in Joseph B. Fabry, Reuven P. Bulka, and William S. Sahakian, eds., *Logotherapy in Action*. Foreword by Viktor E. Frankl (New York: Jason Aronson, 1979).

55. See Viktor E. Frankl, *The Doctor and the Soul* (New York: Knopf, 1965).

56. Rollo May, *Existential Psychology*, 2nd ed. (New York: Random House, 1969).

57. Karl Dienelt, *Von Freud zu Frankl* (Vienna: Österreichischer Bundesverlag, 1967).

58. Note also a statement in the documents of Vatican II: "We are witnesses of the birth of a new humanism, one in which man is defined first of all by his responsibility."

59. May, *Existential Psychology*.

60. F. Gordon Pleune, "All Dis-Ease Is Not Disease," *International Journal of Psycho-Analysis*, 46 (1965), p. 358.

61. E. Mansell Pattison, "Ego Morality," *Psychoanalytic Review*, 55 (1968), pp. 187-222.

62. L. Krasner, quoted in David Grossman, "Of Whose Unscientific Methods and Unaware Values?" *Psychotherapy*, 5 (1968), p. 53.

63. Joseph Wolpe and Arnold A. Lazarus, *Behavior Therapy Techniques* (Oxford, England: Pergamon Press, 1966).

64. Thomas D. Yarnell, "Purpose-in-Life Test: Further Correlates," *Journal of Individual Psychology*, 27 (1971), pp. 76–79.
65. S. Kratochvil and I. Planova.
66. Jann Ruch, (paper presented to the Logotherapy Institute at the United States International University, San Diego, 1973).
67. Joseph A. Durlak, "Relationship between Individual Attitudes toward Life and Death," *Journal of Consulting and Clinical Psychology*, 38 (1972), p. 463.
68. Augustine Meier, "Frankl's 'Will to Meaning' as Measured by the Purpose-in-Life Test in relation to Age and Sex Differences" (Ph.D. dissertation, University of Ottawa, 1973).
69. Leonard Murphy, ("Extent of Purpose-in-Life and Four Frankl-Proposed Life Objectives" (Ph.D. dissertation, University of Ottawa, 1967).
70. Meier, op. cit.
71. "Meaning in Life," *Time*, February 2,1968, pp. 38–40.
72. Nicholas Mosley, *Natalie, Natalia* (New York: Coward, McCann & Geoghegan, 1971).
73. Judd Marmor, "Cancer Counselors," *Time*, vol. 100, no. 7, p. 52.
74. Paul H. Blachly, *Life-Threatening Behavior*.
75. If self-transcendence is denied and the door to meanings and values is closed, reasons and motives are replaced by conditioning processes. This opens the door to manipulation, and it is up to the "hidden persuaders" to do the conditioning, to manipulate man. And vice versa. If one is to manipulate human beings he has to indoctrinate them along the lines of pan-determinism. "Only by dispossessing autonomous man," says B. F. Skinner *(Beyond Freedom and Dignity* [New York: Alfred A. Knopf, 1971])," can we turn to the real causes of human behavior—from the inaccessible to the manipulable." I quite simply think, first of all, that conditioning processes are not the real causes of human behavior; secondly, that its real cause is something accessible, provided that the humanness of human behavior is not denied on a priori

grounds; and, thirdly, that the humanness of human behavior cannot be revealed unless we recognize that the real "cause" of a given individual's behavior is not a cause but, rather, a reason. What, then, is the difference between causes and reasons? If you cut onions you weep. Your tears have a cause. But you have no reason to weep. . . .

76. Joseph Wolpe, "Neurotic Depression," *American Journal of Psychotherapy,* 25 (1971), pp. 362–368.

77. The statement that logotherapy is not a panacea—as much as it might disarm its adversaries—may disappoint its admirers. Edgar Krout of West Georgia College confronted his students with a number of statements quoted from the literature in the field of logotherapy. While there was about 90 percent general agreement with them, some 50 percent of the students were reluctant to credit one of the statements: They did not want to accept the fact that logotherapy is no panacea.

References

Allport, G. W., 1956, *The Individual and His Religion*. New York: Macmillan.

Cannon, B. W., 1932, *The Wisdom of the Body*. New York: W. W. Norton.

Einstein, A., 1950, *Out of My Later Years*. New York: Philosophical Library.

Frankl, V. E., 1938, "Zur geistigen Problematik der Psychotherapie," *Zeitschrift für Psychotherapie* 10:33

Frankl, V. E., 1949, *Der unbedingte Mensch*. Wien.

Frankl, V. E., 1951, "Über Psychotherapie," *Wiener Zeitschrift für Nervenheilkunde* 3:461.

Frankl, V. E., 1955, *Pathologie des Zeitgeistes*. Wien.

Frankl, V. E., 1984a, *Man's Search for Meaning: An Introduction to Logotherapy*. New York: Simon and Schuster.

Frankl, V. E., 1984b, *The Will to Meaning: Foundations and Applications of Logotherapy*. New York: Plume Books, The New American Library.

Frankl, V. E., 1985a, *The Unconscious God: Psychotherapy and Theology*. New York: Simon and Schuster.

Frankl, V. E., 1985b, *The Unheard Cry for Meaning: Psychotherapy and Humanism*. New York: Touchstone Books, Simon and Schuster.

Frankl, V. E., 1985c, *Psychotherapy and Existentialism: Selected Papers on Logotherapy*. New York: Simon and Schuster.

Frankl, V. E., 1986, *The Doctor and the Soul: From Psychotherapy to Logotherapy*. New York: Vintage Books.

James, W., 1897, *The Will to Believe and Other Essays in Popular Philosophy*. New York: Longman.

Lorenz, K., 1981, *Leben ist Lernen*. München.

Moser, G., 1978, *Wie finde ich den Sinn des Lebens?* Freiburg.

Pfister, O., 1904, *Die Willensfreiheit: Eine kritisch-systematische Untersuchung.* Berlin. Quoted in Thomas Bonhoeffer, 1973, "Das Christentum und die Angst—dreissig Jahre später," *Wege zum Menschen* 25(11/12):433.

Wertheimer, M., 1961, "Some Problems in the Theory of Ethics," In M. Henle (editor), *Documents of Gestalt Psychology.* Berkeley: University of California Press.

Wittgenstein, L., 1960, *Tagebücher 1914–16.* Frankfurt a. M.

Yalom, I. D., 1980, *Existential Psychotherapy.* New York: Basic books.

Further Books by Viktor E. Frankl

A listing of all volumes authored by Viktor Frankl, as well as a comprehensive online bibliography on logotherapy, may be accessed at the website of the Viktor Frankl Institute (www.viktorfrankl.org).

The Doctor and the Soul: From Psychotherapy to Logotherapy. Alfred A. Knopf, New York, 1986. Paperback edition: Souvenir, London, 2004.

The Feeling of Meaninglessness—A Challenge to Psychotherapy and Philosophy. Edited and with an Introduction by Alexander Batthyány. Marquette University Press, Milwaukee, 2010; Marquette Studies in Philosophy Vol. 60.

On the Theory and Therapy of Mental Disorders. An Introduction to Logotherapy and Existential Analysis. Translated by James M. DuBois. Routledge, London, 2004.

Man's Search for Meaning. An Introduction to Logotherapy. Rider, London, 2004. Gift edition with additional material, Rider, London, 2011.

The Unheard Cry for Meaning. Psychotherapy and Humanism. Hodder and Stoughton, London, 1988.

Viktor Frankl—Recollections. An Autobiography. Insight Books, Perseus Books Publishing, New York 1997; Paperback edition: Perseus Book Group, New York, 2000.

The Will to Meaning: Foundations and Applications of Logotherapy. New York and Cleveland, The World Publishing Company, 1969. Paperback edition: New American Library, New York, 1989.

Afterword by Alexander Batthyány: Over Thirty-Five Years Later—Research in Logotherapy Since 1975

Since the first English translation of *Man's Search for Ultimate Meaning* was originally published over thirty-five years ago, the body of empirical work in logotherapy and existential analysis and their neighbouring disciplines has grown substantially—so substantially, in fact, that the editors of this book decided to include a brief overview of the recent research in the form of this afterword. Today, the archives at the Viktor Frankl Institute in Vienna, which collects and catalogues research publications on logotherapy, hold some 700 publications (Vesely and Fizzotti 2011), the vast majority of which were published in the mid-1970s or later; of these, about half are clinical or empirical studies in logotherapy or existential analysis.

In 2005, David Guttmann and I (Alexander Batthyány) conducted a search in *PsycInfo*, the Scientific Abstract Service of the *American Psychological Association*, and unearthed 613 studies relevant to logotherapy published in peer-reviewed scientific psychology, psychiatry and medical journals between 1975 and 2005 (Batthyány and Guttmann 2005). Furthermore, a search in spring 2011 in *PsycInfo* revealed that approximately 180 additional studies relating to logotherapy and existential analysis, or, more generally, meaning-oriented psychology, had been published since 2005 alone.

Even from a purely quantitative point of view, these results are impressive, and they clearly demonstrate that existential questions, which Frankl described as being fundamentally bound up with motivation theory, are sufficiently relevant, practical and results-oriented to form the object of empirical research, despite their roots in existential philosophy and psychology. Arguably, this was not apparent when Frankl developed logotherapy and existential analysis in the first half of the last century, nor was it foreseeable in 1975 that logotherapeutic concepts should become as prominent in empirical psychology as these numbers of publications suggest. For example, in his overview of meaning as a psychological factor in the *Handbook of Positive Psychology*, Roy F. Baumeister describes the reception of Frankl's model as follows:

> Psychologists gradually have begun to study meaning in life. Frankl's (1959/1976) early work emphasized the importance of finding value in life, and he is widely credited with being a pioneer in the study of meaning. His work constituted a courageous rebellion against the behaviourist and psycho-dynamic paradigms that dominated psychological theorizing at that time. [. . .] Still, these works were isolated intellectually from the main work of their time (Baumeister and Vohs 2002:608).

William Damon, Jennifer Menon and Karen Bronk see the situation similarly:

> The notion that ethereal constructs such as "meaning" and "purpose" could make a difference—that they could motivate someone to do something, or even shape a person's basic choices about how to live—seemed impossibly soft-headed and sentimental to mainstream psychologists of that time. If

the behaviourist and psychoanalytic schools (the two best-known bodies of psychological work at mid-century) agreed on anything at all, it was that meaning, purpose, and other such belief systems were the products of more fundamental drives; that they were dependent on the drives for their shape, substance, and very existence; and that meaning and purpose were no more than marginal factors in behavioural development. (Damon, Menon and Bronk 2003)

The special, perhaps even isolated, place that Frankl's work occupied for a long time within academic psychology and psychiatry—apart from its endorsement by, for example, other pioneers such as Gordon W. Allport, Alexandra Adler, Hans Eysenck, Elisabeth Kübler-Ross and Sophie Freud—is also reflected in one of the first systematic empirical studies conducted in logotherapy. "An Experimental Investigation in Existentialism" (Crumbaugh and Maholick 1964) was the provocative title of James Crumbaugh and Leonard Maholick's 1964 article in the *Journal of Clinical Psychology*, in which they described their first attempt to investigate the psychological aspects of the will to meaning through their "Purpose-in-Life Test". Existentialism and empirical studies are rarely found in direct association with one another even today, but back in 1964, during the heydays of Skinnerian behaviourism (i.e. the view that mental events can be completely analysed and understood in the form of actual or possible behavioural outputs), it must have seemed an even more curious, perhaps even frivolous, combination. In the (real or apparent) tension between the "empirical" and "existential" camps lies an important key to understanding the place of logotherapy within the empirical behavioural sciences: as a philosophically grounded psychological model which is prepared to leave the comfort zone of armchair philosophy and allow itself to be subjected—indeed, even desires and demands that it be subjected—to empirical scrutiny and clinical outcome studies (Frankl and Fabry 1978).

As can be seen from the research summarized by Frankl in Chapter 8: "New Research in Logotherapy circa 1975", after Crumbaugh and Maholick's pioneering study—and following continuing encouragement from Frankl himself—various researchers both committed to and sceptical of logotherapy's psychological model started to conduct empirical tests on its motivation and personality theory and its clinical efficacy.

The majority of studies conducted on these topics in the years leading up to 1975 aimed first of all to show that the motivation theory of logotherapy—that human beings are essentially searching for a specific and concrete meaning above and beyond any relating to their immediate physical, psychological and social needs and concerns—is coherent and has a high degree of psychological relevance. Taking this a step further, a subsequent group of studies attempted to demonstrate that a temporary or chronic frustration of the will to meaning paves the way for a range of mental disorders and indispositions; or, more specifically, that even if such conditions are presumably the result of multiple factors, a perceived absence of meaning in life significantly increases a patient's susceptibility to neurotic disorders and depressive symptoms.

Conversely, yet another set of studies summarized by Frankl in Chapter 8 shows that a newly found sense of meaning, for example as a result of logotherapeutic intervention, brings with it significantly improved mental health and has a protective effect and, whether in isolation or in conjunction with further therapeutic intervention, is capable of initiating or promoting psychological healing processes. Thus there was already research available in 1975 which showed that logotherapy concepts could withstand empirical testing; however, until just a few years ago, such studies were still usually carried out in a pioneering spirit which sought to test the basic tenets of a psychological (and philosophical) theory that was not yet anywhere near entering the psychological mainstream.

As hinted at above, and as the sheer number of recent psychological studies on the question of meaning shows, this situation has changed significantly in the past few years. One likely factor to have contributed to the growth of interest in existential psychology may be the fact that, from around 1970 on, psychological thinking in general has become more open to new ideas, especially since increasing numbers of academic psychologists have become aware of the limits of orthodox psychoanalysis (Bornstein 2001, Paris 2004). At the same time, behaviourism, which for several decades was particularly strong within experimental psychology, has likewise lost much of its original dominance. Both developments in the history of ideas in psychology took place perhaps largely owing to the so-called 'cognitive turn' in behavioural science (i.e. the move towards scientifically studying and exploring internal mental processes), which soon spread into clinical and experimental psychology (Gardner 1986, Eysenck and Keane 1993).

This "turn" brought with it not only a rediscovery of the central role of internal representations of the world, which logotherapy had identified much earlier as being crucial for understanding human experience and behaviour (Frankl 1958); the increased receptiveness of psychology to less mechanistic or purely psychodynamic models also led to researchers abandoning some of their earlier almost exclusive focus on deficits, and encouraged them instead to look again at those inner resources by which real and apparent deficits can be overcome or regulated in a psychologically mature and healthy way.

Frankl, too, considered much of the "old psy-chologies" to be disproportionately concerned with deficits and limits, and held that—to put it simply—they often tended towards a reductionist pathologism, which attempted to explain even such deeply human and existential concerns as the need for meaning and authenticity not as expressions of human maturity, but as mere compensations for psychological defects and frustrated "lower" needs (Frankl 1961). In brief, for a long time psychology was largely *deficit-based* rather than resource-oriented. Frankl, on the other hand, always placed importance on those inner resources which, even during precarious times in a patient's life, can exert a protective effect in crisis prevention and a curative influence in crisis intervention. He further held that a sense of individual meaning and purpose is the most potent resource of this kind, and in turn also the most effective in activating other psychological resources.

For several decades now, positive psychology has interacted with these ideas on a broad basis (Seligman and Csikszentmihalyi 2000). Again, looking at the positive sides of human existence is not an entirely new idea in the history of scientific psychology: in parallel with Frankl, and as early as in the 1930s, Charlotte Bühler proposed to study not only the life histories of the mentally ill, but also the lives of those individuals who had remained mentally healthy under the same or similar life conditions as the mentally ill, to determine which resources they activated. In other words, she proposed to investigate not just what makes people sick, but also what keeps them healthy (Bühler 1933).

Nevertheless, the systematic scientific pursuit of a broad-based, resource-oriented psychology is a relatively new undertaking and—at least to logotherapists—it can come as no surprise that research in this area was soon to find that meaning is a central psychological (and existential) resource (Klingberg 2009). Indeed, a recent, contemporary review of empirical studies on the will to meaning and its psychological impact since 1975 revealed an immense surge of interest in the topic over the past thirty-five years. For instance, Guttmann and I (2005

Ch. I.1) identified several hundred research articles which corroborate the findings described by Frankl in Chapter 8. These studies use a range of reliable standardized psychometric tests and unanimously support the notion that the will to meaning is a central motivating force that is independent of variables such as gender, age and other demographic factors.

In addition, Steger et al. (2008) conducted three larger studies involving more than 570 participants, in which they used correlation analyses to show that—independently of individual differences such as cognitive style, Big Five personality traits (extraversion, neuroticism, openness, agreeableness and conscientiousness), Big Three (i.e. Positive Emotionality, Negative Emotionality, and Constraint, as well as eleven subscales: Wellbeing, Social Potency, Achievement, Social Closeness, Stress Reaction, Alienation, Aggression, Control, Harm Avoidance, Traditionalism, and Absorption), and Approach-Avoidance tendency (which describe individual differences concerning sensitivity to reward and punishment; Carver and White, 1994)—the search for meaning is a *distinct* psychological factor. In other words, it is not reducible to or derivable from other motivations or variables: "correlations with an extensive array of cognitive and personality measures strongly suggest that the search for meaning in life is distinct from these variables. [. . .] We also used partial correlations to look at the heart of the search for meaning, namely the deep-seated human desire to understand, integrate, and synthesize experience" (ibid.; for similar results see also the mediation analyses in Stillman et al. 2010, Study 2).

Once it has been established that the will to meaning is a fundamental (and irreducible) human motivation, two further areas of research arise. The first relates to the influence that a sense of meaning may have on the development of, or protection against, mental health problems; and the second, in turn, consists in testing logotherapy's prediction that a restored sense of meaning should provide crucial healing and coping resources to patients suffering from mental health issues or the psychological impact of negative life events.

In our research into logotherapy literature, Guttmann and I identified more than 320 studies which address the first question. In these studies, statistically significant correlations between a perceived lack of meaning and a general increase in neuroticism scores or more specific mental health problems (ranging from depressiveness, substance-abuse disorders, eating disorders, anxiety and obsessive-compulsive disorders, phobias, and adjustment disorders) invariably accounted for a relatively large proportion of either the causative mechanisms behind these disorders or the severity of their symptomatologies (*cf.* Batthyány and Guttmann, Chs. II.1 and 2). In fact, frustration of the will to meaning was so strong a predictor of the presence of mental health problems that in their research overview D. Rosenberg and R. Green conclude that "findings indicate the usefulness of the Purpose-in-Life Test for discriminating psychiatric patients from normals in a population" (Rosenberg and Green 1998).

Strictly speaking, however, these findings do not yet support the much stronger prediction of logotherapy— namely, that psychological problems themselves are caused or exacerbated at least to some extent by a perceived lack of meaning in life; for, at first sight, it is equally conceivable that increased neuroticism could bring about a reduced sense of meaning without itself having been the result of a lack of meaning.

Logotherapeutic theories about the impact that a sense of meaninglessness may have on mental health issues were not in fact tested in great detail until relatively recently, when a number of researchers conducted regression analyses and prospective studies on the aetiological role of meaning on psychological distress. Harlow and Newcomb (1990), for instance, used latent variable and structural models, and found that a perceived lack of meaning in life was by far the most significant mediator between subjective loss of control and depression triggered by uncontrollable stressful events, substance abuse in female participants, and self-derogation and suicidal tendency in male participants (see also Harlow, Newcomb and Bentler 1986). Using a similar test design, Kinnier et al. (1994) demonstrated that feelings of meaninglessness were the most significant mediator between depression and substance abuse; in addition, a weak sense of meaning in life emerged in this study as the only significant predictor of substance abuse, and predicted no less than 33 per cent of the variance in substance abuse and addiction disorders.

Daniel Shek (1998) conducted a broad-based prospective longitudinal study among Chinese adolescents and (using a multiple-regression analysis) found that, out of the seven factors tested, the purpose in life scores—followed by self-esteem—ranked first in their significance as predictors of subsequent general psychological mor-bidity. In another prospective longitudinal study, Mascaro and Rosen (2005) showed that meaning in life "explained significant amounts of variance in hope and depressive symptoms two months later beyond the variance explained by baseline levels of hope/depression, neuroticism, conscientiousness, agreeableness, openness to experience, extraversion, and social desirability." In a follow-up study, these authors furthermore found that meaning significantly moderated the relationship between daily stress and depression, leading them to conclude that meaning acts as "a buffer against the effects of stress on well-being" (Mascaro and Rosen 2006).

At least one other prospective study, conducted over a period of fourteen months, found that a strong sense of meaning in life in older participants was a more significant predictor of successful ageing than traditional factors such as social and cognitive resources and other demographic variables (Reker 2002). Hence, both mediation analyses and longitudinal studies suggest that there are clinically relevant correlations between a perceived lack of meaning and mental health problems; moreover, they imply that this relationship is present not only because a sense of meaninglessness may result from poor mental health, but because a weak sense of meaning in life is itself a significant predictor of overall impaired mental health and behaviour.

For several years now, this causal relationship has also been researched intensively in relation to a suicidal tendencies; so intensively, indeed, that one widely used test in suicide research—the Reasons for Living Index (RFL)—is no longer limited, as most earlier tests were, to measuring the intensity and frequency of suicidal impulses, but also includes an index for the reasons *why* patients do not follow their suicidal impulses (Linehan, Goodstein, Nielsen, and Chiles 1983). The RFL has proven to be a reliable and outstandingly predictive test (Malone et al. 2000; Gutierrez et al. 2000; Britton et al. 2008), which is hardly surprising from a logotherapeutic viewpoint. In fact, Frankl used a simplified, heuristic form of this test as early as the late 1930s:

> At first, we pose the question to the respective patient as to whether he still fosters suicidal intentions. In every case [. . .] he will deny our first question; whereupon we submit to him a second question, which almost sounds brutal: *why* does he no longer wish to take his own life? And now it is shown with regularity, that he who genuinely does not harbour suicidal intentions is immediately ready with a series of reasons and counterarguments that all speak against him throwing his own life away: [. . .] that he remains considerate of his family or must think of his professional commitments, that he still has many obligations, etc. Meanwhile, the person who has only dissimulated his

suicidal intentions will be exposed by our second question, and not having an answer for it, react from a position that is characterized by embarrassment on account of the fact that he is at a loss for an argument that would speak against suicide. (Frankl 1947/2010:22)

With regard to the protective and preventive influence that a sense of meaning brings in relation to suicidal impulses, we have already touched upon the second group of studies into the relevance of meaning for mental health. This second group deals with either the restoration of mental health in the course of successful therapeutic intervention, or with its maintenance in the course of successful preventative work during stressful life events. D. L. Debats (1996), for example, found in a large therapeutic follow-up study that "meaning in life (a) affects both positive and negative aspects of well-being, (b) that it is related to improvement during psychotherapy, and (c) that it predicts the outcome of psychotherapy, independently of patients' pre-treatment levels of well-being." Similarly, Waisberg (1993) reports in relation to the results of a three-month course of therapy on patients with alcoholism that "the mean Purpose-in-Life Test (PIL) score before treatment was significantly below the normal range and the mean PIL score at the end of in-patient treatment was within the normal range. Furthermore, the PIL score at the end of treatment was predictive of changes in health at follow-up. It was also predictive of follow-up drinking/drug use status."

Comparable findings demonstrating the curative effect (and predictive value in longitudinal studies) of a strong sense of meaning in life have also been obtained in relation to numerous other groups of disorders: Guttmann and I (2005, Ch. II.1) identified 79 such studies in which a sense of meaning played either a significant role or, where the study design allowed this to be identified, a probable or confirmed primary role in the recovery of patients undergoing psychotherapeutic or psychiatric treatment for a variety of psychological or psychiatric disorders (for earlier reviews, see Kish and Moody 1989 and Zika and Chamberlain 1987, 1992).

Studies looking at the significance of a sense of meaning in the processing of external stresses and traumatic life events yield similar results. Guttmann and I (2005, Ch.I.2) identified more than 150 such studies addressing the role of existential concerns in profound life crises such as illness, grief, and death. Impressive as these figures are, given that the first group of studies referred to above clearly demonstrates that the search for meaning is in any case a deeply human quest, the finding that the search for meaning becomes particularly urgent and prominent in times of personal upheaval does not come as any great surprise. Additionally, quantitative studies are of course not capable of giving due attention to the perhaps more pressing question as to *how* patients might use specific meaning-oriented resources in order to cope with particular kinds of suffering.

A more empirically accessible question is whether people cope with extreme life situations as a result of successfully activating their individual resources of meaning, or by discovering new sources of meaning in spite of, or even because of, their current life circumstances. And, indeed, such a positive relationship has been consistently demonstrated in numerous studies; furthermore, these studies often reveal the considerable impact that a sense of meaning can have on the ability to cope with difficult circumstances. For instance, Bowes, Tamlyn and Butler (2002) found in a study on female patients with advanced ovarian cancer that "the conse-quence of finding meaning in life was a perception of well-being defined by the women as satisfaction with their lives." Conversely, an inability to find meaning in life resulted in feelings of despair, while Lyon and Younger (2001) report that, among a group of 137 AIDS patients observed over a period of several months, a lack of "purpose in life was a stronger predictor of depressive symptoms than was HIV disease severity and [...] was more important than laboratory markers of disease progression for predicting depressive comorbidity."

The positive effect of a sense of meaning, however, is not restricted to alleviating *psychological* pain in the context of chronic or terminal disease. Hence, for instance, studies on chronic pain patients have shown that a sense of meaning correlates not only with significantly lower levels of hopelessness, depression, anxiety and anger, but also that successful completion of logotherapeutic intervention brings about significant improvements in the clinical picture in chronic pain: "A one-year follow-up study [showed that] of 23 adults who had participated in a multimodal treatment program for chronic pain, significant decreases in pain, depression, anxiety, somatisation, hostility, and analgesic ingestion were found without symptom substitution." (Khatami 1987; for similar results, see Kass et al. 1991; Nagata 2003).

With these findings on the impact exerted by existential concerns on psychological and physiological health, not only logotherapy's motivation theory, but also its personality theory comes into focus. For although Frankl is widely recognized as the psychologist and psychiatrist who put meaning on psychology's map, his work has to offer much more than that: the will to meaning, while a central element of logotherapy, is by no means the only one. According to logotherapy, human beings are not only self-transcendent—in other words, open to the world and the meaning that it might hold for them—they are also endowed with a capacity of self-detachment, i.e. logotherapy holds that though we may not be free from our conditions, we are free to determine the type, nature and extent of the effects of these conditions (i.e. relative free will).

This notion, in contrast to logotherapy's motivation theory, initially appeared to be a conjecture or credo, i.e. the belief in an individual's capacity to detach and distance him- or herself from conditions and yet simultaneously determine the nature of his or her impact and influence on those conditions ("the psychotherapeutic credo"—Frankl 1964). However, the concept of self-detachment did not remain mere conjecture for long. For, remarkably, Frankl succeeded in demonstrating the therapeutic efficacy of self-detachment for precisely those groups of patients who experience what appear to be particularly freedom-inhibiting conditions, e.g. anxiety and obsessive-compulsive disorders (OCD).

Specifically, Frankl's method of paradoxical intention (Frankl 1938) is based on what at first sight looks like a relatively simple trick, by which patients can consciously and intentionally disrupt the vicious circle of anticipatory anxiety and anxiety-related and obsessive-compulsive symptoms by (a) acknowledging the non-volitional nature of their overwhelming and irrational feelings, and by (b) refusing to be blackmailed and threatened by these anxious and irrational feelings, and (c) by finally using humorous exaggeration as means to break their spell. In numerous studies (about forty of which are summarized in Batthyány and Guttmann 2005, Ch. II.2.2.) paradoxical intention has been shown to be a particularly effective and fast-working therapeutic technique; in fact, research in this area has demonstrated that self-distancing can reduce symptoms to a similar, and sometimes greater extent than psycho-pharmacotherapy for OCD, for example (Schwartz 1996, 1997b).

Paradoxical intention is perhaps one of the logo-therapeutic techniques whose clinical effectiveness has been investigated most thoroughly, since it was quickly adopted by other psychotherapeutic schools such as cognitive behavioural therapy, which in turn has contributed to its popularity and further clinical testing outside the field of logotherapy (for an overview, see Ascher 2005). Furthermore, novel theoretical models (such as Wegner's ironic processing model; Wegner 1989, Anderson and Green 2001) led to the development of new experimental protocols which are capable of analysing what takes place at a cognitive level when patients temporarily lose conscious control over their experience (for example in anxiety disorder), or their will (for example in OCD; Schwartz 1997a). Many of these models merely express in somewhat different terms (e.g. "ironic" [Wegner 1989] vs. "paradox" [Frankl 1938]) what, long before the cognitive turn, Frankl had proposed was a cause of defective modes of experience and behaviour and which he made successfully treatable using paradoxical intention (and self-detachment).

Additionally, and in line with the evidence for the overall (also physiological) positive effect that a sense of meaning has in the cases cited earlier of chronic pain patients, J.M. Schwartz (1997a and b, 1998) found that self-distancing as a treatment method for OCD not only significantly reduces OCD symptomatology, but also regulates known OCD-specific pathogenetic activity in the orbital frontal cortex within a period of only ten weeks. (For related findings on depressive brooding and hyper-reflection, and the neurologically regulating effects of self-detachment and de-reflection after a period of sixteen weeks, see Kennedy et al. 2007.)

Of course, in addition to its therapeutic and clinical relevance, the evidence of downwards causation via self-detachment clearly has significant philosophical implications, since it strongly corroborates logotherapy's definition of relative free will as a person's ability not only to decide freely how to act vis-à-vis his or her psychological or physiological conditions, but also to form and shape those conditions to such an extent that they are no longer merely manifestations of disease and disorder, but genuine expressions of a person's freedom of choice (i.e. pathogenesis; cf. Frankl 2004). As Schwartz puts it:

> There is one particularly key point, both clinically and philosophically, to comprehend about what occurs at the interface of conscious experience and brain activity during the moments of therapeutic breakthrough in the course of treatment—those moments always involve an *active* process. For at the moment when the man with OCD summons the mental strength to exert his will and physically actualize his new understanding by adaptively changing his behaviour, he will be overcoming tremendous biological forces that are operating in order to resist that change. And the force [. . .] represents the essence of what the words *active* and *purposeful* really mean (Schwartz 1999).

Against the background of these and the other research studies which highlight and corroborate particular aspects of Frankl's logotherapy, it is perhaps important to recall at this point that Frankl did not propose a series of mutually independent psychological hypotheses and therapeutic methods, but rather formulated a highly generative overall psychological model, which forms the basis for the development of logotherapeutic methods. These methods consequently represent both the applied and the applicable (and empirically verifiable) side of the philosophical foundation of logotherapy, i.e. of existential analysis as described in the preceding chapters of this book. The research presented in this afterword and Chapter 8 therefore represent much more than isolated findings and data; rather, when taken together, they complement each other and provide strong evidence in support of logotherapy and existential analysis *as a whole*, i.e. as a philosophically grounded, yet at the same time practice- and outcome-focussed, and hence empirically testable, model of human nature.

As discussed earlier, ties between the existential tradition in psychology, which was initiated largely by Frankl, and experimental psychology and cognitive research have only been forged in the last few years. And yet the extent to which the empirically and clinically testable predictions of logotherapy and existential analysis have been confirmed during this short period by numerous researchers working independently from one another, using different methods, and different evaluation techniques, is truly remarkable.

So where are we now, some thirty-five years after *Man's Search for Ultimate Meaning* was first translated into English? Even if restrictions of space allow only for a short overview of recent research in logotherapy and existential analysis in these pages, it appears as if Frankl's logotherapy—once a single psychiatrist's "courageous rebellion against the [. . .] paradigms that dominated psychological theorizing" (Baumeister and Vohs 2002)—has now, albeit belatedly, arrived at the forefront of research in the fields of experimental, empirical and clinical psychology.

ALEXANDER BATTHYÁNY

Alexander Batthyány teaches Philosophy of Psychology and Cognitive Science at the University of Vienna, and Logotherapy and Existential Analysis at Vienna Medical School. He is the Director and Head of the Research Department at the Viktor Frankl Institute, Vienna and Editor of the fourteen-volume edition of the *Collected Works of Viktor Frankl*. He has published several books, book chapters and articles on philosophical psychology, the contemporary philosophy of mind, and logotherapy and existential analysis.

A note from Alexander Batthyány: With thanks to my colleague David Guttmann for our collaboration on much of the research the appendix is based upon, and Hugh Fraser and Sue Lascelles for their help with the English version of it.

References

Anderson, M. C. and Green, C. (2001). Suppressing Unwanted Memories by Executive Control. *Nature*, 410

Ascher, M. L. (2005). Paradoxical Intention and Related Techniques. In: Freeman, A., Felgoise, S.H., Nezu, C., Nezu, A. M., Reinecke, M. A. (Eds.) (2005). *Encyclopedia of Cognitive Behavior Therapy*. New York: Springer

Batthyány, A. and Guttmann, D. (2005). *Empirical Research in Logotherapy and Meaning-Oriented Psychotherapy*. Phoenix, AZ: Zeig, Tucker and Theisen

Batthyány, A. and Levinson, J. (Eds.) (2009). *Existential Psychotherapy of Meaning: Handbook of Logotherapy and Existential Analysis*. Phoenix, AZ: Zeig, Tucker and Theisen

Baumeister, R. and Vohs, K. (2002). *The Pursuit of Meaningfulness in Life*. In: Snyder, C. and Lopez, J. (Eds.). (2002). *Handbook of Positive Psychology*. Oxford: Oxford University Press

Bornstein, R. F. (2001). The Impending Death of Psychoanalysis. *Psychoanalytic Psychology*, 18:3

Bowes, D. E., Tamlyn, D. and Butler L. J. (2002). Women living with ovarian cancer: Dealing with an early death. *Health Care for Women International*, 23:2

Britton, P. C., Duberstein, P. R., Conner, K. R., Heisel, M. J., Hirsch, J. K., Conwell, Y. (2008). Reasons for Living, Hopelessness, and Suicide Ideation Among Depressed Adults 50 Years or Older. *American Journal of Geriatric Psychiatry*, 16:9

Bühler, Charlotte (1933). *Der menschliche Lebenslauf als psychologisches Problem*. Leipzig: Hirzel

Carver, C. S., Sutton, S. K. and Scheier, M. F. (2000). Action, Emotion, and Personality: Emerging Conceptual Integration. *Personality and Social Psychology Bulletin*, 26

Crumbaugh, J. C. and Maholick, L. T. (1964). An Experimental Study in Existentialism: The Psychometric Approach to Frankl's Concept of Noögenic Neurosis. *Journal of Clinical Psychology*, 20

Damon, W., Menon, J. and Bronk, K. C. (2003). The Development of Purpose During Adolescence. *Applied Developmental Science*, 7:3

Debats, D. L. (1996). Meaning in Life: Clinical Relevance and Predictive Power. *Journal of Clinical Psychology*, 35:4

Eysenck, M. W. and Keane, M. T. (1993) *Cognitive Psychology*, London: Lawrence Erlbaum

Fizzotti, E. and Vesely, F., Online Bibliography on Logotherapy and Existential Analysis, www.viktorfrankl.org/e/bibE.html

Frankl, V. E. and Fabry, J. B. (1978-1979). Aspects and Prospects of Logotherapy: A Dialogue with Viktor Frankl. *The International Forum for Logotherapy Journal of Search for Meaning*, 2

Frankl, V. E. (1958). *Existential Analysis and Logotherapy*. In: Frankl, V.E. (2010)

Frankl, V. E. (1960). *Beyond Self-Actualization and Self-Expression*. In: Frankl, V. E. (2010)

Frankl, V. E. (1961). Philosophical Basis of Psychotherapy. *Philosophy Today*, 5:59–64

Frankl, V. E. (1964). *The Concept of Man in Logotherapy*. In: Frankl, V. E. (2010)

Frankl, V. E. (2004). *On the Theory and Therapy of Mental Disorders*. Translated and with an Introduction by James M. DuBois. London: Routledge.

Frankl, V.E. (2010). *The Feeling of Meaninglessness. A Challenge to Psychotherapy and Philosophy*. Edited and with an Introduction by Alexander Batthyány. Milwaukee: Marquette University Press

Gardner, H. (1986). *The Mind's New Science : A History of the Cognitive Revolution*. New York: Basic Books

Graybiel, A. and Rauch, S. (2000). Toward a Neurobiology of Obsessive-Compulsive Disorder. *Neuron*, 28

Gutierrez, P. M., Osman, A., Kopper, B. A.; Barrios, F. X. (2000). Why Young People do not Kill Themselves: The Reasons for Living Inventory for Adolescents. *Journal of Clinical Child Psychology*, 29:2

Harlow, L. L., Newcomb, M. D. and Bentler, P. M. (1986). Depression, Self-Derogation, Substance Abuse, and Suicide Ideation: Lack of Purpose in Life as a Mediational Factor. *Journal of Clinical Psychology*, 42

Harlow, L. L. and Newcomb, M. D. (1990). Towards a general hierarchical model of meaning and satisfaction in life. *Multivariate Behavioral Research*, 25:3

Kass, J. D., Friedman, R., Leserman, J. and Caudill, M. (1991). An Inventory of Positive Psychological Attitudes with Potential Relevance to Health Outcomes: Validation and Preliminary Testing. *Behavioral Medicine*, 17:3

Kennedy, S. H., Konarski, J. Z., Segal, V. Z., Lau, M. A., Bieling, P. J., McIntyre, R. S. and Mayberg, S. L. (2007). Differences in Brain Glucose Metabolism Between Responders to CBT and Venlafaxine in a 16-Week Randomized Controlled Trial. *American Journal of Psychiatry*, 7:164

Khatami, M. (1987). Logotherapy for Chronic Pain. *International Forum for Logotherapy*, 10:2

Kish, G. and Moody, D. (1989). Psychopathology and Life Purpose. *International Journal of Logotherapy*, 12:1

Kinnier, R. T., Metha, A. T., Keim, J. S., Okey, J. L., Alder-Tabia, R. L., Berry, M. A. and Mulvenon, S. W. (1994). Depression, Meaninglessness, and Substance Abuse in "Normal" and Hospitalized Adolescents. *Journal of Alcohol and Drug Education*, 39:2

Klingberg, H. (2009). Logotherapy, Frankl, and Positive Psychology. In: Batthyány, A. and Levinson, J. (2009)

Linehan, M. M., Goodstein, J. L., Nielsen. S. L. and Chiles, J. A. (1983). Reasons for Staying Alive when you are Thinking of Killing Yourself: The Reasons for Living Inventory. *Journal of Consulting and Clinical Psychology*, 51

Lyon, D. E. and Younger, J. B. (2001). Purpose in life and depressive symptoms in persons living with HIV disease. *Journal of Nursing Scholarship*, 33:2

Malone, K., Oquendo, M., Haas, G. L., Ellis, S. P., Li, S. and Mann, J. J. (2000). Protective Factors Against Suicidal Acts in Major Depression: Reasons for Living. *American Journal of Psychiatry*, 157:2

Mascaro, N. and Rosen, D. H. (2005). Existential Meaning's Role in the Enhancement of Hope and Prevention of Depressive Symptoms. *Journal of Personality*, 73, 985–1014

Mascaro, N. and Rosen, D. H. (2006). The Role of Existential Meaning as a Buffer against Stress. *Journal of Humanistic Psychology*, 46, 168–190

Nagata, K. (2003). A Study of Logotherapy for Chronic Low Back Pain Patients. *Seishin Shinkeigaku Zasshi*, 105:4

Paris, J. (2004). *The Fall of an Icon: Psychoanalysis and Academic Psychiatry*. Toronto: University of Toronto Press

Reker, G. T. (2002). Prospective Predictors of Successful Aging in Community-

Residing and Institutionalized Canadian Elderly. *Ageing International*, 27

Rosenberg, D. and Green, R. (1998). Meaning and Mental Health. A Review of the PIL: Validity, Reliability and Predictive Value. *Journal of Psychometric Research*, 22:1

Schwartz, J. M. (1997a). Cognitive-Behavioral Self-Treatment for Obsessive-Compulsive Disorder Systematically Alters Cerebral Metabolism. In: Hollander, E. and Stein, D. J. (Eds.) (1997). *Obsessive-Compulsive Disorders: Diagnosis, Etiology, Treatment*. New York: Marcel Dekker

Schwartz, J. M. (1997b). Obsessive-Compulsive Disorder. *Science and Medicine*, 4:2

Schwartz, J. M. (1998). Neuroanatomical Aspects of Cognitive-Behavioural Therapy Response in Obsessive-Compulsive Disorder: An Evolving Perspective on Brain and Behaviour. *British Journal of Psychiatry*, 173 (suppl. 35)

Schwartz, J. M. (1999). First Steps toward a Theory of Mental Force: PET Imaging of Systematic Cerebral Changes after Psychological Treatment of Obsessive-Compulsive Disorder. In: *Toward a Science of Consciousness*. Boston: MIT CogNet

Schwartz, J. M. (1996). Systematic Changes in Cerebral Glucose Metabolic Rate after Successful Behavior Modification Treatment of Obsessive-Compulsive Disorder. *Archives of General Psychiatry*, 53: 109-113

Seligman, M. E. P. and Csikszentmihalyi, M. (2000). Positive Psychology: An Introduction. *American Psychologist*, 55 (1): 5–14

Shek, D. T. (1998). Adolescent Positive Mental Health and Psychological Symptoms: A Longitudinal Study in a Chinese Context. *Psychologia: An International Journal of Psychology in the Orient*. 41:4

Steger, M. F., Kashdan, T. B., Sullivan, B. A. and Lorentz, D. (2008). Understanding the Search for Meaning in Life: Personality, Cognitive Style, and the Dynamic Between Seeking and Experiencing Meaning. *Journal of Personality*, 76:2

Stillman, T., Lambert, N. M., Fincham, F. D. and Baumeister, R. F. (2010). Meaning as Magnetic Force: Evidence That Meaning in Life Promotes Interpersonal Appeal. *Social Psychological and Personality Science*, 8:10

Waisberg, J. L. (1994) Purpose in Life and Outcome of Treatment for Alcohol Dependence. *British Journal of Clinical Psychology*, 33:1

Wegner, D. (1989). *White Bears and Other Unwanted Thoughts: Suppression, Obsession and the Psychology of Mental Control*. New York: Viking.

Zika, S. and Chamberlain, K. (1987). Relation of Hassles and Personality to Subjective Well-Being. *Journal of Personality and Social Psychology*, 53.

Zika, S. and Chamberlain, K. (1992). On the Relation Between Meaning in Life and Psychological Well-Being. *British Journal of Psychology*, 83.

Index

189